CITY PLANNING

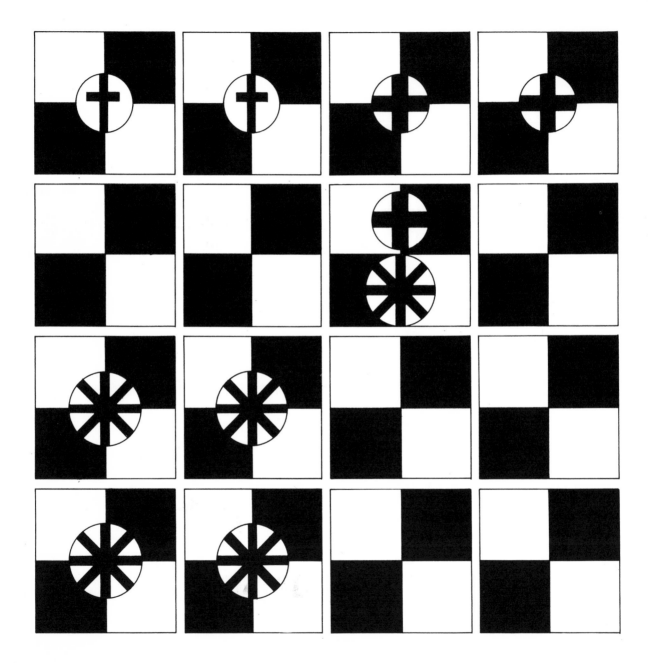

CITY PLANNING

the games of human settlement

Forrest Wilson

 VAN NOSTRAND REINHOLD COMPANY

NEW YORK CINCINNATI TORONTO LONDON MELBOURNE

To Betty, Jonathan, Robert, and Paul

Van Nostrand Reinhold Company Regional Offices:
New York Cincinnati Chicago Millbrae Dallas
Van Nostrand Reinhold Company International Offices:
London Toronto Melbourne

Copyright (c) 1975 by Litton Educational Publishing, Inc.
Library of Congress Catalog Card Number 73-1625
ISBN 0-442-29513-8

Published by Van Nostrand Reinhold Company
A Division of Litton Educational Publishing, Inc.
450 West 33rd Street, New York, N.Y. 10001

16 15 14 13 12 11 10 9 8 7 6 5 4 3 2 1

Library of Congress Cataloging in Publication Data

Wilson, Forrest, 1918-
  City planning

  Bibliography: p.
  1. Cities and towns — Planning — Study and teaching.
2. Cities and towns — Planning — Simulation methods.
3. Educational games. I. Title.
HT166.W568   309.2'62   73-1625
ISBN 0-442-29513-8

Contents

Introduction

People live together in many ways. There are ordered rows of houses and straight streets, like the disciplined camps of soldiers, or confused jumbles of houses connected by winding paths where everyone builds as he pleases. But the configuration of every human settlement, ordered or haphazard, has reasons for its particular form.

If we watched a campground from its beginning, we would understand these reasons as the human settlement took shape. The first campers select their sites to suit themselves. As more and more people gather, the original haphazard confusion gives way to a semblance of order. The campers begin to use certain spaces for specialized activities. There are public spaces for vehicles, such as roads and parking places, communal spaces are set aside around a well or pump, and a location is found for the public toilets. The campers will also select a place for playing ball, and meeting places to talk, play, or sing. As people gather together into settlements, you will find that they plan an arrangement of public and private spaces.

The form of a human settlement reveals the customs, habits, and social ideas of the people living there. The games people play with their lives are revealed by the form of their settlement. It tells us by its size, shape, and arrangement which human actions are encouraged and which are not.

The shape of our surroundings physically obstructs, encourages, and directs our actions. Built form has a common meaning to all men in all periods of their history despite their cultural differences.

Row houses designed for factory workers during the latter part of the eighteenth century.

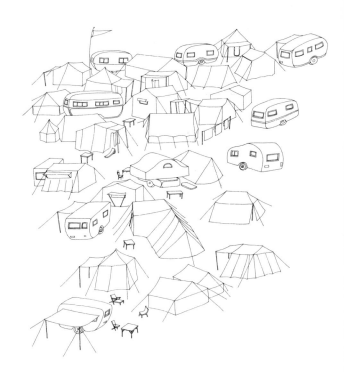

Plan of a street in a mobile home park, today.

6

There are three clearly identifiable scales that give man a sense of place in his built environment. The smallest is that of objects such as furniture which gently suggest how we should arrange ourselves for certain actions. Then there is the shape of rooms which permits and obstructs the human actions that take place within them. On the largest scale, that of the human settlement, the arrangement of buildings presents monumental barriers and compelling directives in the spaces which they generate. Similar geometric forms suggest similar human actions no matter what their size. People gather around a round table, are drawn to the center of a round room, or assemble in the middle of a round plaza. The forms of human settlements are therefore clues to human actions, which we can interpret from our own personal experiences.

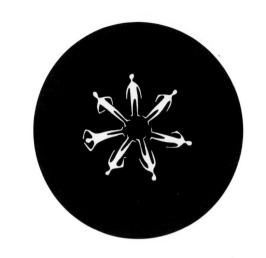

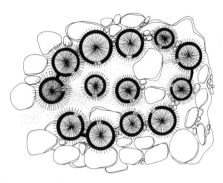

Plan of an African village.

Drawings of human settlements are called plans. These diagram a settlement as if we were looking down upon it from a high place and could see it all at once. The patterns of squares, rectangles, and circles, of straight and squiggly lines, can be translated into streets, houses, and buildings, public and private spaces. The plan of a village, town, or city is a record of the kinds of social, economic, religious, political, and human relationships which have developed among its inhabitants.

Plan of thruway traffic-change cloverleaf, today.

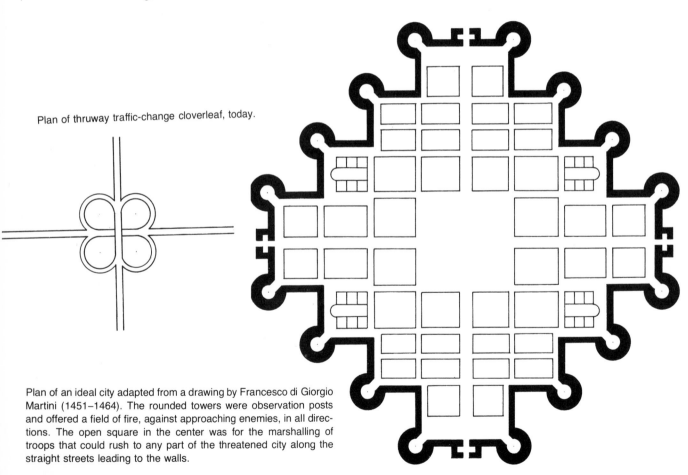

Plan of an ideal city adapted from a drawing by Francesco di Giorgio Martini (1451–1464). The rounded towers were observation posts and offered a field of fire, against approaching enemies, in all directions. The open square in the center was for the marshalling of troops that could rush to any part of the threatened city along the straight streets leading to the walls.

One human activity is a function of, that is, depends on, another. If one is changed, so are the others. Human settlements have hundreds of these interrelated functions. For example, if people fear attack, they will cluster together and build strong walls around themselves, or they will build on a high cliff, on stilts over the water, or on some other inaccessible place. Inaccessibility of the human settlement is therefore a function of fear. If buildings are spread out and easily accessible, people feel secure. An open plan is a function of security.

Man takes nature's materials and builds shelters to temper the natural environment. No matter where or how he lives, he must arrange his buildings in some manner. The important thing is the choices he makes and why they are made.

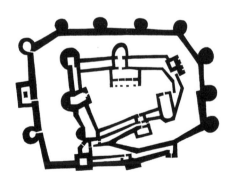

Plan of the walls, towers, and inner defenses of a medieval crusader castle built in Syria.

The Games

Most of the games in this book are designed to develop the physical form of a human settlement as the game is played. To do this it will be necessary to make cardboard cutouts representing the buildings of each settlement.

The gaming board represents the land upon which people gain their living and upon which the buildings are built.

The playing pieces are cut out of cardboard following the drawings shown in the book. The plan of the village should be drawn on a large sheet of wrapping paper or cardboard.

The size can be determined by the number of players. The playing pieces should be drawn upon cheap cardboard and cut out with either a matt knife or scissors. They should be scored with a ball-point pen or other pointed but dull instrument, to make them fold easier.

The size of the playing pieces is determined by their relation to the playing board. They do not have to be exact and can be colored or marked to make them look more realistic and to distinguish each player's pieces.

A white glue should be used to fasten the cardboard together. Hold the pieces in your fingers or secure them with clothespins until they dry. They will usually stick together by themselves in three or four minutes. They should then be allowed to dry for another five or ten minutes.

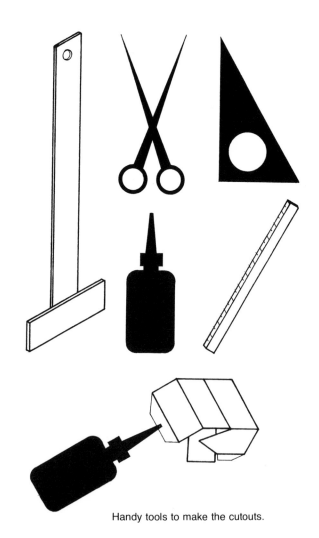

Handy tools to make the cutouts.

The Gaming Plan of Human Settlements

People gather together for security or common religious, political, or economic interests. Their settlements are places for the production of goods and services. They are also places where people live, study, play, work, and have children. They may be places of magic or terror, beauty or ugliness. If they are crowded and noisy, they are successful; for when human settlements fail, they are abandoned.

Villages and cities conform to the games people play with their lives. When we can identify the rules by which people live, the form of both the smallest village and the largest city is understandable.

When a human settlement is viewed as a game, the rules approximate the physical, political, economic, and social environment within which human actions take place.

A game is defined by its rules; these include the players, their number, what they can do, their value systems, the available choices, and their rewards. Certain moves are allowed for certain conditions and are forbidden for others.

The games that are found in this book do not give all the rules affecting the human settlements described. They do, however, approximate the general conditions and the dominant laws and customs that helped to determine the settlement's physical form.

Human settlements with set rules have a characteristic physical form. It is only when people change the economic, religious, political, and social laws and customs they live by that new settlements are born, existing settlements change, and old ones die.

The Stone Age Mobile Home

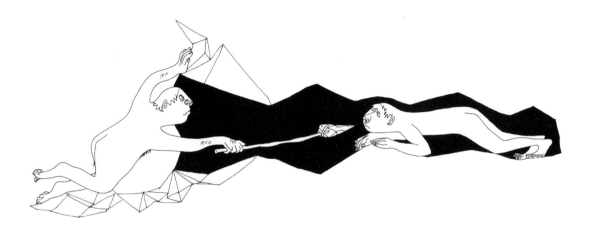

The hunters of the early stone ages did not stay in one place long enough to build permanent settlements. A hunting life will sustain less than ten people per square mile, and stone-age hunters had to cover every inch of it in their restless search for food. The animals they killed were quickly eaten. Early man feasted and starved in turn. His stomach was his storehouse, refrigerator, and deep freeze.

Primitive man was a free-roaming individual who crept and stalked about with throwing stick, club, and spear. He was a clever tool-maker and skillful hunter but not too adept at social organization. There is ample evidence that he killed and ate other men as well as wild animals.

Man the hunter led a life not much different from that of the animals he pursued and which occasionally pursued him. His life was a precarious adventure determined by the laws of chance.

His quest for food was a never-ending search. As a result, man learned to eat anything that grew, walked, ran, crawled, flew, or swam. His menu consisted of fruits, roots, insects, lizards, frogs, birds, rats, mice, fish, and any larger animal he could dispatch.

Venison was the most common of all food. The many species of deer, antelope, and gazelle made this the most important food of pre-agricultural times. This staple was sometimes varied by more exotic fare as evidenced by the refuse heaps left by early hunters all over the world. On Mount Carmel they ate hippopotamus. In Kenya the diet featured zebra and baboon, and in China, ostrich eggs. The residue around prehistoric Texas cooking fires shows that Neolithic Texans ate coyote, prairie dogs, and rabbits. Stone-age hunters recognized members of their own species as edible. They had an enormously varied menu; its variety made up for what it often lacked in quantity.

When man began to eat grasses and cereals, it marked the end of his hunting life. With grain on his menu he had a food supply that could be grown and stored. He was no longer dependent on food that had to be eaten immediately. Permanent settlements were a function of cereal food.

Early man's environmental protective devices were as adaptable as his taste buds. He used skins for clothing and anything not edible for shelter. Enclosures were made of tropical leaves, skins, twigs, boughs, timbers, stone, earth, turf, and even whale and mammoth bones.

Hunters are usually not major property owners; they keep only what they can carry in their travels. Tools and weapons were more valuable to early hunters than the temporary homes they constructed.

Early man built in the jungle, on mountain slopes and prairies, by rivers and the seashore, in swamps, and over water. He left garbage and the wreckage of his houses wherever he traveled. These leavings are evidence that he traveled everywhere.

Houses were erected individually, in clusters, or as one large communal structure. Yet as long as early man remained a hunter, his settlements were never large or permanent. He never stayed in one place long enough to become a permanent home owner.

Stone age hunters were often glad to accept the solid shelter of natural caves and overhanging rocks and cliffs. But there seems to be no positive proof, and there is even some doubt, that caves and rock shelters were man's first choice of a home.

The first free-roaming hunters did not use caves except when cold drove them into any shelter they could find. They remained footloose wanderers, building windbreaks or light coverings against rain and sun as they were needed.

Fire was used for warmth, protection against wild beasts, and for hardening wooden tools and weapons, long before it was used for cooking. At first, fire was probably not kindled, but used and preserved when

found. Once fire was mastered, man could use caves. The cave was a function of fire.

Cave dwellers lived on top of their refuse. In some cases bones and other rubbish accumulated to such an extent that the cave itself was almost filled.

The largest stone-age garbage heaps have been discovered in the caves of southwest Europe, although similar traces of early man have been found in Kenya, along the shores of the Mediterranean, in China, and in North America, indicating that although stone-age man was not neat he was widely traveled.

Domestic life of the cave centered just inside the cave mouth. Here the cave dwellers used daylight to work and escaped the smoke of the great fires essential for cave life. The cave depths were used only for religious and hunting rituals. Neolithic man showed a natural preference for caves facing south and westward even as architects site houses today.

In the cave region of southwest France, cave dwellings have been found within sight and calling distance of each other. Although they may not all have been occupied at one time, there seems evidence that a number of people used them simultaneously. These were perhaps the first temporarily permanent human settlements although they remained merely way-stations in the never-ending hunt for food.

The game that describes the life of early man is one of movement and chance. He left us no conclusive settlement forms. He left only broken tools, refuse, bones, and occasionally magnificent art in the depths of his caves to mark the temporary halts in his restless search for food.

The Hunting-Gathering Game

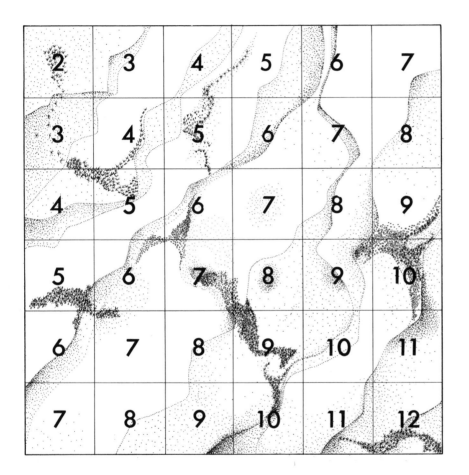

This is a game about the hunting trip of several bands of primitive hunters. The objective of the game is to go to the hunting ground, hunt for a week, and then return with as much game as possible. The winner is the player who catches the most game and loses the fewest hunters.

Materials

A pair of dice, a number of beans, peas, or any small objects that can be used as markers to represent hunters on the gaming board. Eight of these are required for each player. A square sheet of paper at least 12" and preferably larger is needed for a gaming board. The paper is marked into 36 squares, 6 vertical and 6 horizontal. If the paper is 12", the squares will be 2"; if 18", they will be 3", and so on. The larger the paper, the larger the squares. Mark the squares with the numbers as shown on the drawing.

You now have a gaming board that is a matrix of the number combinations possible with two dice. It also represents the terrain over which the hunters will range in their search for game.

Players

Any number of people can play. If more than two enter the game, they should start after the first two groups have left their camp. If the game is played by one player, the object is survival. He should return with at least one point for each day the hunting party has been gone to make the trip worthwhile.

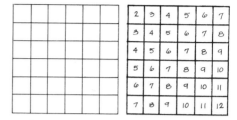

Rules

1. Each player has eight hunters represented by beans or other markers.

2. Players begin at 2 or 12. They throw the dice for odd or even numbers. They can only move horizontally or vertically on the trip to the hunting ground. The hunting ground is the territory marked by the squares 6, 7, and 8.

3. The player moves to an odd or even number if it is adjacent to his square and he throws an odd or even number during his turn with the dice. The objective is to move from 2 or 12 to the hunting ground. Points can only be scored in the squares 6, 7, 8. If the player throws a 6 or an 8 during his trip to the hunting ground, he may go directly there.

4. Once the hunting ground is reached, each hunting party begins to hunt. Players roll the dice in turn. The number that comes up represents the game he finds in the square he occupies. After each throw for an animal he must move to another square within the hunting ground.

5. Each player stays in the hunting ground for seven rounds of play and then returns to either 2 or 12. Points are then tallied. The winner is the hunting party that returns with the most points and the most hunters.

6. After the seventh play in the hunting ground each player must return to the square from which he started. He cannot hunt for game, even if he is still in the hunting square.

7. If more than two people play, they must begin at intervals from the 2 and 12 squares. They can only hunt in the hunting ground.

8. The numbers on the dice correspond to the animals on the drawings. After each throw the score is recorded and the dice are passed to the next player. The player must move to another square in the hunting ground for each turn.

2	3	4	5	6	7
3	4	5	6	7	8
4	5	6	7	8	9
5	6	7	8	9	10
6	7	8	9	10	11
7	8	9	10	11	12

9. Double numbers count double. For example, a mammoth (6 and 6), will count for twice 12, that is, 24. The rhinoceros (5 and 5), will count 20, and so on. For man (1 and 1), however, there is a special condition. These rules apply to hunting parties of eight and larger.

10. The value of killing a saber-toothed tiger (3 and 4), is 14 points, but, like man (1 and 1), there is a special condition.

11. When the player finds himself in a square with either a saber-toothed tiger (3 and 4), or man (1 and 1), he throws the dice three times. If he gets another 3 and 4 or 1 and 1, he has killed the tiger or the man and collects the points. If he does not, but throws the number of an adjacent square, his hunting party can retreat from the danger and suffer a day without food. However, if the player fails to score either the man, the tiger, or the number of an adjacent square, he must stay where he is and lose two of his players. He must await his next turn to see if his luck changes.

12. Each player in turn has three rolls to move to another square in the hunting territory. He must throw either a 6, 7, or 8 and then moves to that square. If he throws the same number as the one he occupies, he moves diagonally to the next square of the same number.

13. Players must move their hunters no matter what number they throw if it is an adjacent square. The first number to appear is the numbered square they must choose.

14. If the hunting band has been reduced to six hunters, they must consider the double 6 as they would the tiger and man: that is, kill the animal or lose hunters. If the party has been reduced to four, it must also consider the double 5 as well as the double 6 dangerous animals. If the band has been reduced to two hunters, they must run from all double numbers with no possibility of scoring. A hunting party of two that meets man or tiger is automatically lost.

When the hunters encounter man, it is probably best to retreat. Man is dangerous and not very good eating anyway. It is also probably best to retreat when the player encounters a saber-toothed tiger. It is very possible that primitive hunters spent their entire lifetime without enjoying a tiger steak. However, the same cannot be said for the tiger about man steaks.

The Odds

If you look at the matrix of dice numbers on the gaming board, you will see the frequency with which numbers occur. For example, it is easy to see that there is only one 2 and one 12 and that there are six combinations of 7, and five of both 6 and 8, and so on.

We assume that the dice are fair and that there is no more reason for them to roll one way than another. If we consider the throw of a single die (the singular of dice is a die) any one of its faces may turn up. Therefore, the chances of throwing a 1, 2, 3, 4, 5, or 6 are all equal.

If we want to know the chance of throwing a 5, we can see that it is the ratio of the number of successful ways to the total number of faces on the die. That is, there is one chance in six or 1/6. If we wanted to know the chance of throwing a number over 3, that is, 4, 5, or 6, it would be 3/6 or 50 percent.

If you look at the gaming board or the chart, you will see that there are 36 different ways the dice can come face up, beginning with double 1 and ending with double 6. The chance of throwing any number is simply the frequency that that number can be thrown, over 36. The chance of throwing a 7, which has six combinations, is 6/36 or 1/6 or 16.66 percent.

If the player looks at the chart, counts the number of possibilities, and divides them by 36, he can judge the percentage odds of each play and decide on his chances.

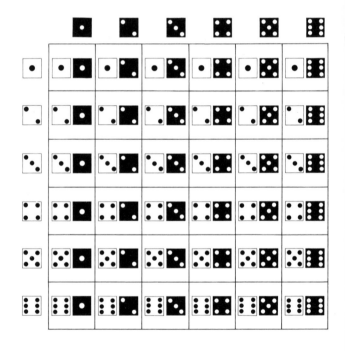

Prehistoric Settlements

We know that prehistoric man planned his settlements because we find primitive people living today under much the same conditions as they did in the distant past. They have clearly defined ways of arranging their buildings. Social relationships determine the positioning of the structures.

Hunting tribes maintain physical mobility and free personal relationships. Their shelters are arranged with a maximum of flexibility and a minimum of formal planning. The more settled a group becomes and the more emphasis they place on land and property, the more inclined they are to arrange their buildings in fixed patterns.

As an economic surplus accumulates, social and religious laws and customs become more complicated. With the accumulation of wealth there is an increase in the distinctions between groups. Poverty is shared, wealth is individual.

An affluent settlement will have privileged positions set aside for the dwelling places of important people, such as merchants, and the chief's warriors and priests, as well as meeting houses for select groups.

We usually think of societies progressing from nomadic hunters and gatherers, to village farmers, and then to city builders; but this is not necessarily so. The dominating factor is the need for food and security.

The Plains Indians of North America are a good example of a culture that exchanged a settled farming life for that of nomadic hunting. The pressure of westward-moving European settlers forced the Indians out of their farming communities. At the same time the Indians acquired rifles and horses. They changed from peaceful farmers to warlike nomadic horsemen in a little over a hundred years. The mounted Indian hunter, equipped with a rifle, could pursue buffalo across the plains and carry back enough meat for his tribe to survive during the severest winter.

Peaceful village life was abandoned for the nomadic life of the buffalo hunter. As the European settlers encroached more and more on the Indian's hunting grounds and wantonly destroyed the buffalo, the Plains Indians became increasingly warlike. It was this cultural reversal that cost General Custer a fine head of hair at Little Big Horn.

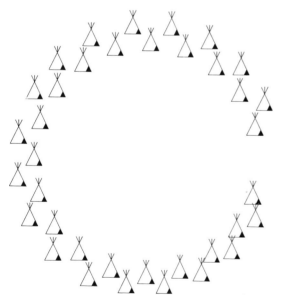

To primitive people the individual shelter is not an isolated structure as it is to us. To them each dwelling is part of the entire settlement and the settlement part of the natural universe. They site their shelters in conformity with natural phenomena. For example, the association of the east and the sunrise with the renewal of life, and the association of the west with the sunset and death are almost universal in primitive societies.

The nomadic Plains Indians arranged their tipis in a fixed plan, a large circular C-shaped ring with the openings toward the east so that the rising sun, symbolizing birth and life, shone into their tipis. As the tribe moved, the Indian leaders camped at either side of the opening facing toward the east. On the return journey the leaders became the rear guard and the opening was reversed to face the previous day's line of march. If the journey was a hunt or raid in which life was to be taken, the opening of the circle faced west. The imaginary course was then toward the sunset, which symbolized the land of the dead.

From the beginnings of time the circle has always held a mystic significance for man. As a reflection of the dome of the sky, it was considered the perfect enclosing form. The center of the primitive villager's universe is the center of his village located in the center of the universal world in the center of the sky.

The greatest pyramid ever built by man, that of Teotihaucan in the valley of Mexico, symbolized for its builders the world's navel at the exact center of the world.

African tribes surround the chief's compound with circles of huts and cattle pens. The important people of the tribe cluster in the center; around them the ring of huts of the commoners pen in the livestock and form a defensive outer fortification.

For primitive people the central public space is the site of the communal campfire and the place of sacred religious rites, feasts, and celebrations. When an African Pygmy talks from his own doorway, he is speaking for himself. If he stands in mid-camp, he is taking the viewpoint of the entire group. The center expresses the idea of solidarity and overall authority.

In primitive settlements the siting of each individual structure has vital significance to its occupant and the settlement as a whole. It is only civilized man that lives in cities out of touch with the sunrise and the sunset, the east-west axis, and the birth and death cycle of the seasons. He locates his buildings without regard for the circular earth, the bowl of the sky, the moon and sun, or the natural order of the earth. Modern man orders his structures according to his earthbound interests. He sets them next to waterways or coal mines for power. He arranges them along highways for transportation or sets his houses in the rigid squares arranged by building developers. His reasons for arranging his settlements are not dictated by nature but the practical demands of an industrialized world. Before we move on to the cities of our time let us look at a primitive agricultural community.

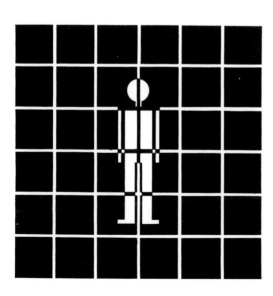

Settlements

Fifteen thousand years ago or thereabouts, man began to adapt his living patterns to a fixed food supply. He stopped running after elusive game and settled in a spot where ocean shellfish were plentiful, or freshwater fish were readily snared in a nearby stream. He varied this diet with roots and game from the nearby woods. With a steady food supply, man had time to clear land, plant, and domesticate animals.

Villages grew and with them a new way of life. The settlement became a permanent gathering of houses, graneries, storage pits, families, neighbors, birds, dogs, pigs, and cattle.

The friendly dog and pig scavenged amid the closely packed community dwellings and each successive generation left its garbage to fertilize the earth for the next. The village and its land was a rich compost heap. The abundant refuse and manure fertilized the fields. Wild grasses eaten and ejected grew in the village manure and mutated to corn. The settlements used up free land but in turn made the remaining land more fertile. But the size of the settlement was limited. A balance always exists between population and soil fertility. As the village became more populated, farmers had to travel longer and longer distances to tend their fields. Eventually the settlement had more people than the land could support. Some of the villagers would then gather together and move to a new site and establish a new village. Villages grew and divided themselves like this for centuries.

Eventually, new economic, social, and political relationships developed. Manufacture, slavery, industry, and piracy produced other forms of wealth as villages grew to cities.

Before we pass on to a growth of cities we will stop to look at a primitive African village in which life is probably much the same as it was in man's first agricultural communities.

The Primitive Village

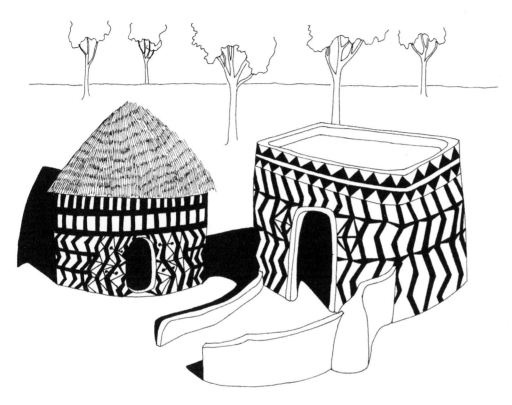

When we speak of primitive buildings, we refer to structures by builders who have been called primitive by archaeologists. This does not mean that the buildings themselves are primitively built. They are often sophisticated in design and succeed in controlling climatic conditions much more successfully than do the buildings of civilized societies.

There are, however, certain building techniques that most primitive builders have in common. There is no universal measuring system — spaces are measured with arms and legs. The power source is the muscles of men and animals. Men, women, and children help in building and all know how a settlement should be planned. Materials are usually scarce but close at hand. Nature and climatic conditions are carefully observed and the builder has an exact knowledge of materials and their properties. He modifies structures and changes plans according to his personal experiences over long periods of time.

Primitive man regards nature as awesome and dominant. He does not make a sharp division between man and animal. Animals are often housed in close proximity to living quarters and sometimes in the house itself. Before primitive man kills an animal for food, cuts down a tree, or removes a rock from the earth, he asks its spirit for forgiveness.

On the compound farms the most actively exploited land surrounds the compound itself, close to its walls. The greater soil fertility in the proximity of the compound dwellings is clearly marked by the gradually increasing height and greenery of the stalks of grain as the compound is approached. Beyond this garden plot there are fields under continual cultivation, fertilized with animal and human manure.

These fields gradually fade out into unmanured croplands as one leaves the village. A crop will be grown and the land left fallow until it naturally refertilizes itself.

Each family group lives within a separate village compound. Each is a separate economic unit. It may consist of a father, all or some of his married or unmarried sons, and their wives, children, and dependents. It may also be composed of brothers and their wives and children, farming together after the father dies.

When civilized man describes architecture, he usually speaks only of spaces enclosed within walls. But for primitive man, building space is extended by trees and rocks. The arrangement of building masses and natural landmarks defines village spaces. Buildings and the settlement itself are the visible expression of the relative importance attached to the different aspects of life. A house is not only shelter but also a symbolic marking of the builder's place in the community — establishing the owner's social and economic importance.

An individual compound of a single family group within the village will begin with the construction of basic housing units built near those of the closest family group of the builder.

The one-room huts may be arranged around an internal court and connected by exterior walls which completely enclose the compound.

Each wife may have her own sleeping room and live with the older girls and young children. Household activities are a cooperative effort supervised by the senior wife.

In some primitive societies a man may have more than one wife, and each wife may be entitled to her own room within the compound. The number of wives a man can support depends upon his age, status, and wealth. The number of buildings in the compound serves as an index of the man's wealth and status.

The family is continually changing, growing, dividing, dispersing, or dissolving. Family growth is marked by the addition of new room units and the extension of walls separating rooms in the compound. Division within a family may not necessarily require the construction of a separate compound at a new location.

The existing compound may simply be altered through reassignment and reorganization of the spaces within it. Only when family divisions establish a new economic unit by the allocation of separate farmlands will a new elementary compound be established.

Animals, humans, and farmland constitute a self-sufficient community. Seldom is there a large enough surplus for trading or selling. People are born, crops are planted and harvested, animals and people refertilize the land. Animals eat the scraps, and are eventually eaten themselves — in a cycle of birth, growth, death, and rebirth.

The African Village Game

The African village game is the game of how a village grows. The objective is to build the largest and most prosperous compound in the village. This can be done by trading and speculating in either animals or land. The players bargain for advantages with each other in trading land, grain, and arranging marriages between their children. All decisions are ultimately affected by natural phenomena. If the player has chosen luckily, he will be affected less by such natural disasters as diseases among the animals or crop failures.

The size of each player's compound is the scorecard. If families prosper, their compounds grow. If they have bad luck, they diminish or may disappear entirely, in which case the player is out of the game.

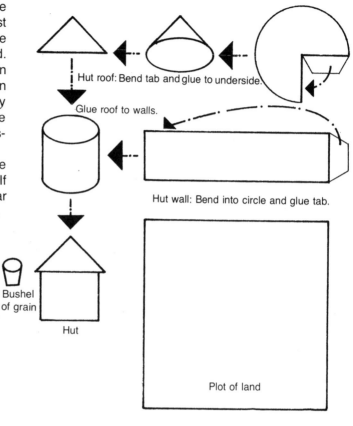

Hut roof: Bend tab and glue to underside.

Glue roof to walls.

Hut wall: Bend into circle and glue tab.

Plot of land

Cows   Goats   Pigs Chickens   Bushel of grain

Man and son   Woman and daughter

Hut

Materials

A pair of dice, a number of strips of light cardboard or heavy paper, and white glue. Cut the strips ¾″ wide and 4″ long as shown on the drawings. They should be glued together as shown. These will be the hut walls. Cut out the semicircular shapes as shown and bend them for the hut roofs. The pieces of cardboard or paper of various shapes and colors are used to indicate livestock and people. Beans, dry peas, or poker chips may be used instead — or any markers the players find convenient. The plots of land should be about 4″ square, to be placed around each player's compound.

Players

The game may be played by two or more players. One player must act as banker. He gives out land, livestock, and people at the beginning of the game; he keeps score of the various transactions; he awards or collects the various markers indicating people, land, animals, and houses according to the rules of the game.

Rules

1. The game is played by rolling dice. You can see from the chart that there are 21 possible combinations beginning with 1 and 1 and ending with 6 and 6.

2. Each play consists of one role of the dice. Dice are rolled by the scorekeeper.

3. The number combination on the dice indicates the happenings during that particular year (see the game card on page 32).

4. After each roll, the scorekeeper awards prizes and collects penalties. The players then have a bargaining session. When it is completed, the dice are rolled again for the next play.

5. Each player begins with a man and his wife, a bull and a cow, two pigs, two goats, ten chickens, and a plot of land. They begin with a three-room compound. The village is composed of the compounds of each player.

6. After each play a child is born for every man and wife. For every two cows, add one calf; for every two pigs or goats, add four piglets and four kids; and for every two chickens, add ten chicks.

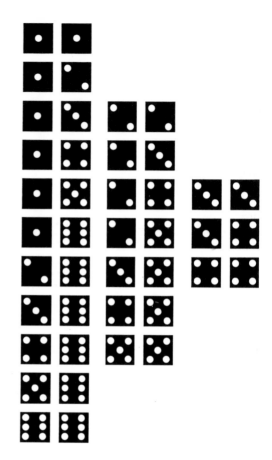

7. After every 15 plays, the children grow to maturity and may marry children from other compounds. The girls go to the compound of the boy's father. He must pay a dowry to the family of the girl.

8. Compound owners can have more than one wife. If a new wife is added to the compound, one chamber is added. If a son marries and brings home his wife, two chambers are added. It is assumed that the children are born alternately boy, girl, boy, girl, etc.

9. When a compound owner wishes to buy a wife for himself or one of his sons, he must pay about six cows or twelve pigs or goats or sixty chickens. But the dowry may be more or less; it is negotiable.

10. After 35 plays the original man and his wife die. Their houses are taken down and the compound rearranged. The oldest son then becomes the compound owner.

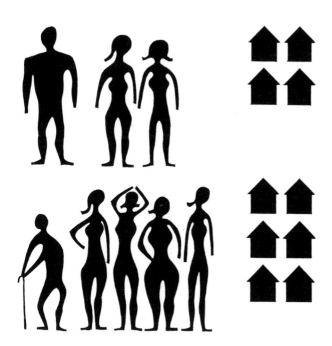

11. The amount of land owned by a compound depends upon the number of inhabitants. A man and his wife have two plots. A man with five wives has four plots. Two additional wives equal one plot of land. When a son grows to maturity, marries, and joins the compound, he is given a plot of land which is added to the land of his compound.

12. Every year (one play) each mature person eats half a cow, one pig, one goat, and ten chickens — or an equivalent amount of grain. Count each child as half a mature person. Each year a good crop means that the compound owner raises enough grain to feed his family or trade for animals. In a normal year each plot of land will yield twenty bushels of grain. One person eats ten bushels of grain a year, or twenty bushels if he does not eat meat.

13. If the compound owner has more land, he trades the excess grain for animals.

14. The dice combination will affect the entire village but will have different meanings for each compound owner. Each player will exercise his own choices. Some will try to acquire wealth in land and others in livestock.

15. Each player must arrange the lives of his compound members to the best advantage in order to be prosperous. If a player cannot arrange a marriage, his son or daughter will become an old maid or bachelor. Children must marry before the age of 25. The compound owner may, therefore, choose to increase or decrease the dowry asked or paid.

Game Card

1-1 — A good harvest year.

1-2 — A drought. The harvest is poor. Meat is eaten instead of grain. Every member of the compound eats twice as many animals as they would normally.

1-3 — A median harvest year. Only enough food for eating is grown; there is none to trade.

2-2 — A good harvest year.

1-4 — Locusts destroy all of the crops. Every family eats twice as much meat, or trades meat for grain to survive.

2-3 — An exceptionally good harvest year. Twice as much is grown. Every plot of land pays double.

1-5 — A good harvest year but disease kills one quarter of the animals in every compound.

2-4 — A good harvest year.

3-3 — Drought. There are no crops and in all compounds half the cows, pigs, and goats die.

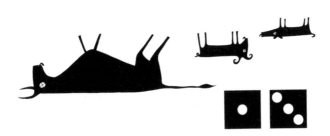

3-5 — The locusts return but eat only half the crops. Each piece of land pays only half.

4-4 — Cholera strikes the village. One of every three children dies.

3-6 — A good harvest year.

4-5 — A good harvest year.

4-6 — A poor harvest year; each plot of land yields only half.

5-5 — Drought, no crops.

5-6 — A good harvest year.

6-6 — A bumper crop; all land pays double.

1-6 — A good harvest year but a chicken disease kills one quarter of all chickens.

2-5 — A good harvest year.

3-4 — A good harvest year.

2-6 — An exceptionally good harvest year; twice as much is grown. Each plot of land pays double.

City Beginnings

When we contrast a primitive farming village with a hunting tribe, we find that the conditions of the fight for survival have changed but nature still dominates. When a village grows into a city, the activities of the inhabitants become specialized. Their lives are no longer dominated by the whims of nature. The blacksmith and the shoemaker are only indirectly affected by animal disease or drought. The merchant is dependent upon his dealings with men. His survival does not depend on his hunting luck or a good crop year.

City dwellers have different rules than either hunters or farmers. A village cannot grow into a city unless its inhabitants outgrow their village ideas and change the rules of how they live together.

The transformation from village to city can be seen taking place in many rural settlements strung out along the highways between today's cities. There are only a few houses at first. One of them might be a combined service station and store. As more people move into the area, their houses join those of the original settlers. At some point the appearance of the houses change. The service station sells groceries and household items. Then some of the original houses begin to cut store windows in their fronts and hang signs above their porches. Their backyards are paved over for parking lots and stores are constructed among the houses.

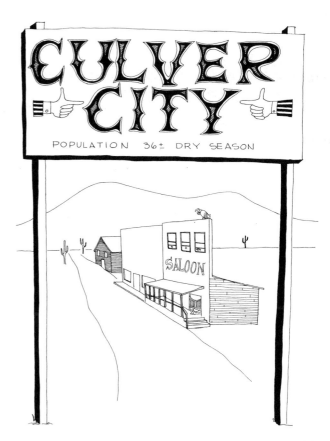

CULVER CITY

POPULATION 36± DRY SEASON

SALOON

The original townspeople move back from the highway and side roads are built. As the original roadside cluster becomes a business district, the surrounding farmland now becomes tract housing. Food is no longer grown on local farms and in local gardens; it is bought by the inhabitants in their local supermarket. The village has changed into a town. Commercial enterprises will support more people than farming, so the settlement grows in density.

As the roadside farming community changes to a town, the ideas of the townsmen must change with it. They must develop different ideas about family life and strangers. A farm family has close family ties. Strangers and outsiders are suspect. In contrast, strangers are the livelihood of the businessman. Every outsider is a potential customer. Eventually the pressure of new ideas changes the outlook of the townspeople. If their ideas do not change — and with them the rules that govern their living together — the settlement will not grow, or conflicts between the inhabitants will destroy it.

There are certain buildings which mark the change from roadside cluster to town. Stores, banks, supermarkets, and service stations are not built unless there are enough people to use them and enough commercial activity to support them. When we see stores and banks, we know we are in a town.

Cities as we know them evolved slowly from closed, baronial strongholds into the walled medieval town. City walls were fashioned to withstand bows, arrows, and battering rams. It was not until the invention of gunpowder that they were lowered and finally disappeared. Walled cities ceased to be built when they were no longer a defense against the weapons used against them.

The adaptability of cities to new conditions is not always predictable. To a certain point stronger walls were the answer to stronger weapons. When weapons changed in concept, however, city walls did not meet the challenge but instead disappeared. The answer to such devastating weapons was attack, mobile armies, or peace.

The fate of the cities themselves could not have been foretold. At the height of the power of the great city-states of Italy it seemed that future human settlements would follow the pattern of independent cities. Gunpowder and cannon which made city walls no longer useful also subjected the independent city governments to national domination. The city as an independent unit became as obsolete as the sword and lance. Following the same reasoning we might indeed ponder if the atom bomb has not made nations obsolete.

The Death and Rebirth of European Cities

The conflicting forces within a city are seldom stabilized. The people that occupy a human settlement are in constant movement. As their needs press them, they press against each other and the city's confines. If the city does not respond, they either shatter its restrictive boundaries or abandon it.

European settlements after the fall of Rome and the loss of the Mediterranean were hardly cities at all. They had been deprived of their vital city functions. For a city to thrive it must be the mixing vessel for a rich diversity of people and ideas. Money is a great common denominator because it has no ideologies; thus, trade and commerce know no boundaries — they vitalize and stimulate human interaction wherever they can thrive.

As the Moslems consolidated their domination of the Mediterranean, their fleets sailed it in complete mastery. They devastated the coasts of France and Italy, put towns to the torch, captured their inhabitants, and sold them into slavery.

Western Europe, which had drawn its sustenance from trade with the East across the Mediterranean, was forced to live in isolation. Religious sentiment, literature and language, and political and social institutions changed as the civilization of the ninth century broke completely with antiquity. Europe became a barbaric and isolated inland kingdom — a closed state, without foreign contact or markets.

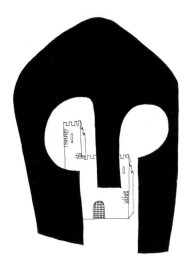

The efforts of Charlemagne to protect the coasts from Saracen raiders were as impotent as his attempts to oppose the invasion of the Norsemen. The Danes and Norwegians easily plundered the coasts of Europe. Every accessible river was an avenue inviting systematic and persistent pillage. The devastation was so complete that in many areas the population disappeared. Inland Europe was unable to organize the defense of its coasts against either Saracens or Norsemen.

Europe suffered a falling off of trade and wealth. Gold coinage was abandoned and silver was substituted in its place. The state itself could not retain its monopoly of minting coins. The Roman poll tax no longer existed. The sovereign's resources consisted only of tributes levied on conquered tribes, war booty, and the return from his lands.

The state was unable to pay tax collectors, bailiffs, or governors, and was therefore unable to control them. It was forced to share its power with the aristocracy, a group whose best interests were served by diminishing the power of the state. The central government, theoretically dominant, was in fact dependent upon the fidelity of its hostile, independent nobles.

The financial weakness which accompanied the decline of the inland empire was a clear demonstration of the state's inability to maintain a political structure without the benefit of trade or commerce. Its economic base could no longer support the load of a central government. The small independent farmer was squeezed between the estates of the lords and the clergy, without protection.

The land of free farmers was acquired by landed proprietors. Farmers became cultivators bound to the soil from father to son. Their need for protection inevitably made them turn to the powerful lords. They subordinated themselves and their possessions in return for his protection.

The cities had provided a market for the produce of the great estates. When trade ceased, the great estate owners had nowhere to sell their surplus. They ceased to produce more than the minimum they needed for survival. The economy of commerce and exchange disappeared. Each estate constituted a small world, living by and for itself.

The rights of the peasants were heavily restricted by the lord of the manor. To him, the peasants were serfs with no legal right to leave their holdings. They were forced to grind their corn at the lord's mill, they worked his fields for nothing, and they could not give their children in marriage without his consent.

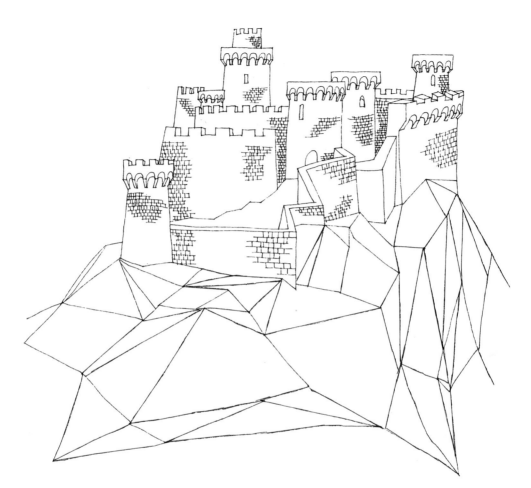

The centers of cultural life in this period of urban stagnation were the great monasteries. The abbey of Saint-Denis was more important at this time than the nearby town of Paris.

The lords used the ancient cities as fortified settlements from which to dominate the surrounding countryside. A few merchants lived outside the walls to serve the court and its attendants. The towns were no longer productive manufacturing centers. They were only consumers.

This world turned in upon itself was solidified into intransigent warring elements. The walled enclosure was typical of human settlements, whether they were castles or fortified abbeys. Stone fortresses stood on the hills while the serfs huddled in wattle and daub hovels at their base. The noble, his family, and his fighting men were quartered within protective stone walls — the serfs were expendable outsiders.

The wealth of lord, king, and churchman lay in the land they controlled. The nations that are now Europe were at one time a checkerboard of warring feudal domains, with each lord savagely contesting against his neighbor and all contesting against the king.

The Game of Warring Castles

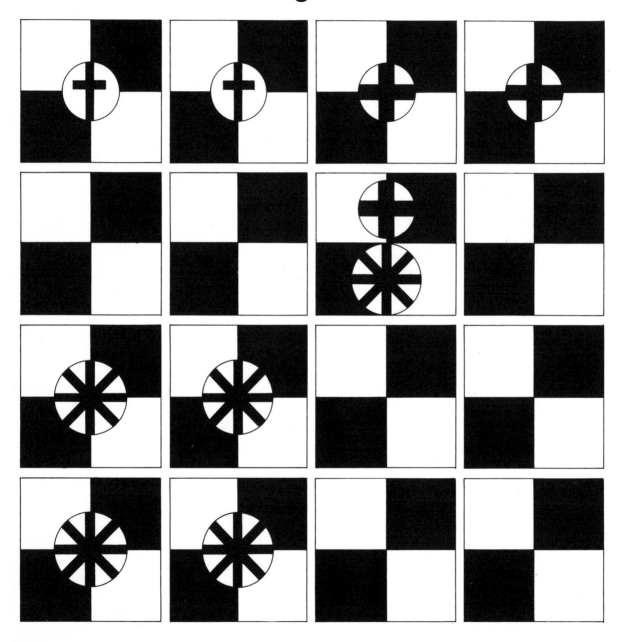

This game is a simulation of conditions before the age of chivalry. It is a game of negotiations, pacts, alliances, and broken treaties. Force rules, and land represents power. When one player feels he can conquer another, he may attack. Treaties can be broken or kept at will. It is a game that represents the contest for power after the death of European cities. The game is between players surrounded by enemies and cut off from the outside world. The sword and the power of armed men predominate.

Cut round circles of cardboard and mark them as shown to represent the noble, churchman, and king. These will be moved on the board much the same as checkers are used on a checkerboard.

Noble   Churchman   King

Materials

A pair of dice. A special checkerboard with paper markers as shown in the drawing. Mark out the checkerboard on a large piece of cardboard at least 24″ x 24″ square. The size of the board will depend upon the number of players.

Players

The game may be played by three or more people. It consists of the king, nobles, and churchmen. There can only be one king but there can be two or three churchmen, and as many nobles as there are squares left on the board. The board does not have to be filled.

Each player has his own color and markers are made as shown.

Rules

1. The objective of each player is to rule the board. The king has more power than one noble or churchman but not as much as two.

2. Each player begins with one square divided into four parts. The king has a square and a half. Placement of pieces indicates the amount of territory held. If the player is in the center, he owns all four segments of the square. If he is on a half, he owns one half and if he is in a corner, he owns only that corner. As players amass more than one square of land, they place their markers on the additional squares.

3. Land represents strength. But squares must be next to each other to count as part of a player's domain.

4. The dice are thrown for numbers as they are in the hunting game. The chart of the hunting game (see page 20) indicates the odds.

5. When a player attacks another, the outcome is decided by rolling the dice. He may attack only his neighbors because land that is not connected does not count as part of his strength.

6. In a contest between players, the one with the most land has the most chances of winning. An attacker with twice as much land as his neighbor has two chances to his opponent's one. The odds are determined and the dice are rolled to decide the outcome of the contest. For example, if a player has twice as much land as his neighbor, he wins if he throws a 7 and loses

if he throws a 10. There are six combinations of 7 and only three of 10. If the players are equally matched, that is, both have the same amount of land, then the point may be 6 and 8. If the player throws a 6, he wins, if an 8, his opponent is victorious. If the contest is between a player with four times the amount of land as another, then 9 and 12 can be used. (Consult the description of odds at the end of the first game.) You will see that there is an equal chance to throw a 6 and an 8 — five combinations of 6 and five combinations of 8 — which makes the odds even. There are six combinations of 7 and three of 10; therefore, the odds are two to one in favor of throwing a 7.

7. When a large landowner attacks a small one, the larger landowner rolls the dice.

8. Contesting players with equal land have equal chances. Each player throws the dice; the one with the highest number throws the dice to decide the outcome of the battle.

9. A player contesting against one with less land can win all of his opponent's land. A small landowner engaging a large landowner in battle is entitled to win only the amount of his own holdings. For example, a full square contesting against a square and one half can only win a full square. If he wins, however, he can immediately attack again with the improved odds of two squares against one half or four to one.

10. When a player loses his land, he is out of the game.

11. The game begins with a negotiation period of ten minutes, in which the players assess their positions. They can negotiate with other players for advantages and disadvantages. They can make alliances, pacts, and treaties either openly or secretly. At the end of the negotiation period the players throw the dice. The one with the highest number is allowed to put his plan into operation first. He is followed by the player with the next highest number, and so on down the line.

12. A round of play is completed when all the players have contested against each other. After each round, the dice are thrown again for high numbers for the next sequence of plays.

13. Two players can band together against a third and combine their land and hence their odds against him. If the former win, they divide their winnings as they have agreed. If the latter wins, he takes half of the amount of land contested from each of his attackers, or all from one, as he chooses.

14. If all the squares are not owned, players adjacent to free squares may contest against each other for the free land between them. When their lands adjoin, they can then contest against each other.

15. The church has land but does not have armed men. The king or a noble may give the church land in return for its support against a rival.

16. The church cannot fight; it must get the king or a noble to fight for it. It lends them the strength of its land to increase odds in their battles against each other. The church then shares in the division of the conquered player's lands according to the pact it made with its ally. If the church is on the losing side, it loses its land.

17. If a noble fights against the king and takes his land, he is then the king.

In the beginning, the king has the initial advantage because he has the most land. If the king elects to attack, the one attacked can either fight back or become the king's vassal. The king then has the extra strength of his vassal, but the vassal remains a vassal only as long as it suits him. He may make an open or secret alliance against the king and attack him when the odds of winning are better.

The church does not have armed men, but it has land. Someone must do its fighting for it. The church may organize the nobles against the king or side with the king against the nobles, but the churchman must have a noble to fight for him.

The king and the nobles use force, the church uses guile. If the church succeeds in defeating all of the nobles but one, the church wins if it has more land than this one surviving player.

The king or noble wins when he has taken the land of all the other nobles and has more land than the church. If they both have an equal amount of land, the noble or king wins.

If the king or noble wins, he is excommunicated but he is the ruler of the land. If the church wins, a Christian kingdom has been established.

If two churchmen band together to defeat the king, they must have nobles to fight for them. They must then get their nobles to contest for them against each other for sole possession of the board. If there are two churchmen and one surviving noble, the noble must fight with one churchman against the other until only one survives.

The game is one of negotiation, guile, force, and deceit — the prize is a nation.

The Medieval Town

By the middle of the eleventh century trade had begun its slow revival, causing the fortresses of churchman and noble alike to crumble away. The Norsemen had settled down in Normandy, and Europe was gathering strength for the Crusades against the Mohammedans. The embryonic medieval city was pushing against the confines of its shell to free itself from feudal domination.

Crossroads, formerly the battlegrounds of iron-armed and ironclad men, were beginning to widen and change into marketplaces which would eventually grow into towns. Nobles were beginning to find more profit in taxation than in war-making.

But all towns were not born from trade. Some came into being through military colonization. A conquering lord might encourage his subjects to live in fortified enclosures on subjugated lands, and to defend them for him. The new settlers were both farmers and militiamen. In protecting themselves, they assured the territorial rights of their lord.

When such conditions occurred, feudal ties were strained. The new settlers were free to move, to sell their goods as they chose and, if threatened, even to fight against their own lord.

The town became the living place of citizens bound together to protect their rights. They fought, bought, and plotted for the right to hold their own markets, to have their own laws, to bear arms, to coin their own money, to establish weights and measures, and to police their own city. Each townsman bore the responsibility for exercising these rights and was willing and able to take up arms to defend them. The new cities were a source of revenue for the feudal lords, but the citizens were a threat to the feudal system.

The city offered an alternative to the serf's life of bondage. He became a free man inside the city walls. The town had independent economic power and weapons for its own defense. Its citizen armies had far more to defend than the lord's mercenaries.

When the feudal lord had to finance his army, when he needed money to join the Crusades or purchase the new luxuries that the merchants were bringing to Europe, his only source of revenue was his land. But he could not sell his land. He could only give grants of autonomy. He could also encourage the growth of settlements which would increase his annual rents. His hands held the sword but the townspeople held the purse strings.

In addition to rents, the lord could extract other income from the towns. He could collect tolls from bridges, local markets, and customs posts. He also benefitted from court fines. These revenues multiplied as the town increased in population. Yet the larger the town became, the more it posed a threat. The feudal

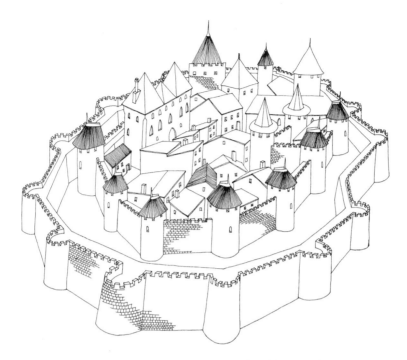

lord was squeezed between his authority and his avarice. The lord did not relinquish his feudal privileges easily. His word was as good as his military strength. The weaker his army, the stronger his word.

The city walls of medieval towns were built on the Roman model. Their design was dictated by military necessity. Walls had three parts — wall, tower, and gate. They were 10 to 20 feet thick and 30 to 60 feet high and were perforated by small openings that provided the garrison a maximum field of cross fire against an attacking enemy. They were designed to be as short in length as possible; for, the shorter the wall, the easier it was to build and the easier to defend.

Walls were solid at the base and wide enough on top to permit the passage of two armed men. Towers projected beyond the line of the wall so that an enemy assaulting the wall was exposed to the fire of missiles on his sides. The distance separating towers was de-termined first by the range of crossbows and bows and arrows and later by the range of firearms.

Towers were round to give a view of the enemy from many points. There were no angles in the wall which could shelter attackers from the missiles of the defenders.

It was also important that walls not be easily approached. Roads leading to towns were designed with steep inclines and approached the town gate from right to left. Soldiers carried their shields on their left arms, and thus presented their exposed sides to the town's defenders as they approached the gate.

In medieval times people tried to get into cities instead of out of them as they do today. Citizens had a special legal status and the closer one could get to the center of the city and its urban activity, the better. But even the periphery just inside the city walls was better than being left outside entirely.

CITY SPACE

Two opposing interests competed for the space within medieval towns. Individuals needed space for the production of goods, for trade, and for living quarters. Trade was the first consideration, living arrangements were secondary. The medieval craftsman lived where he worked. There was no economic justification for separating the two activities.

There are public and private spaces within a city. Public space is by definition accessible to all. Private space, whether enclosed or open, cannot be encroached upon without the consent of the owner.

The medieval town needed public space. The town's vitality depended upon the free movement of buyer and seller.

Besides the city's inhabitants, there were people who came to the city to do business, who owned no private space within it. These were people such as the peasant who came to sell his produce and the wandering trader and craftsman who needed space to sell their wares. The entire town was a market. Trade, production, buying, and selling took place in all of its areas.

There were locations within the medieval town where those who needed public space concentrated. By their very number and vitality they forced the city to widen the space around them. Once a peasant entered the city there was no reason for him to continue to its center; he came there to sell his produce. He stopped his cart just inside the gate and began to sell. As others joined him, a market was born. The pressure of the market gradually forced private space on either side to give way. The street would be widened and a fountain installed. All those who either bought or sold marketed goods and those who made their living from market activities would be attracted. Money lenders and notaries would erect stalls and even a small chapel might be built to service the market.

The struggle for public and private space determined the internal form of the medieval city. The irregular

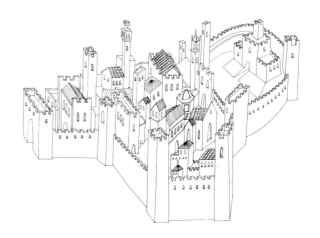

development of streets and markets indicated the political power of groups of individuals competing within the community for the acquisition of private space.

MEDIEVAL SUBURBS

The medieval city grew around its gateways much the same as cities grow around our airports. Today's airline terminal has developed two conflicting functions. It sells tickets, checks baggage, and dispatches passengers as quickly as possible. In reality, however, passengers seldom pass quickly through it. Much time is wasted due to airplane delays or simply in checking in and arranging flights.

Most major airports have restaurants, shops, bars, and barber shops; lounges and hotels have been built nearby. The airport begins to serve as a suburban center as well as a gateway to the city. Nearby suburbanites visit its restaurants and city dwellers themselves make plans to dine there.

The entrance to a medieval city was a waiting place much like an airport. It was here that strangers were inspected, carts were examined, and gate tolls — which were a major form of medieval city income — were collected.

As people congregated around the gates, business began to be done outside the city as well as inside. The townspeople would come out to buy; perhaps an inn would be built for those who had to wait until the next day to get into the city.

Small settlements outside the city gates mushroomed. As the favored positions within the city disappeared, buyers and sellers turned to the markets outside the gates. Markets grew and soon turned into major centers of economic life, as highway shopping centers do today.

As the communities outside the gates grew and gained economic power, they acquired the political strength to demand that the city walls be expanded to include them. If they were successful, the city walls would be enlarged to include the new communities.

Abandoned walls left standing within the city represented a sort of public space which could be encroached upon. The poorer of the town's inhabitants squatted in its ruins, the richer bought the towers and turned them into housing. Houses were built against, through, and over the walls.

The medieval city prospered because of its industrious inhabitants, but the land upon which it was built belonged to the lords. The feudal system of land ownership lasted through the birth, life, and death of medieval towns.

Only a few medieval cities became independent; the fortified residences of the lords and churchmen remained a significant and characteristic part of the others.

The lords were neither craftsmen nor merchants. They were voracious parasites doing little to improve the life of the city, while living on its revenues. As a consequence, the interests of the townsmen and the lords were in constant conflict, and often involved open warfare.

Medieval Town Game

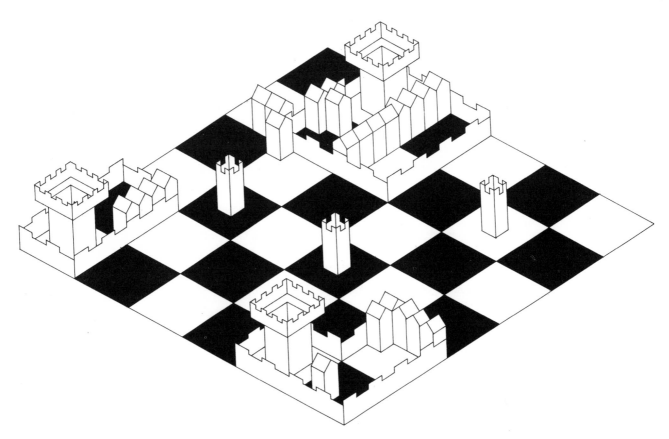

Gaming board and playing pieces

This is a game of lords and merchants. The lords contest against each other and exploit the merchants. The merchants make money in the town and wait for an opportunity to take over the city.

Materials

A pair of dice. Make a checkerboard as shown in the drawings. It can be enlarged for more players. Make the squares any size, the larger the better. They must be able to hold the cutout cardboard castles, towers, and merchant's houses as shown in the drawings. Make the wall sections to fit the squares, and the castles, towers, and merchant's houses in the sizes shown in relation to the size of the squares. Each player may make his pieces a different color or make all the pieces the same color and use marks to identify the different players. The merchants can also mark their houses with their own marks.

Use beans, poker chips, or make markers to represent soldiers. These must be small enough to fit inside the castles and towers.

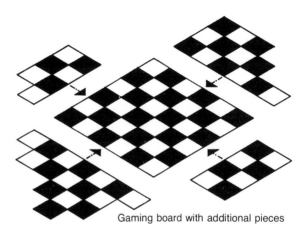

Gaming board with additional pieces

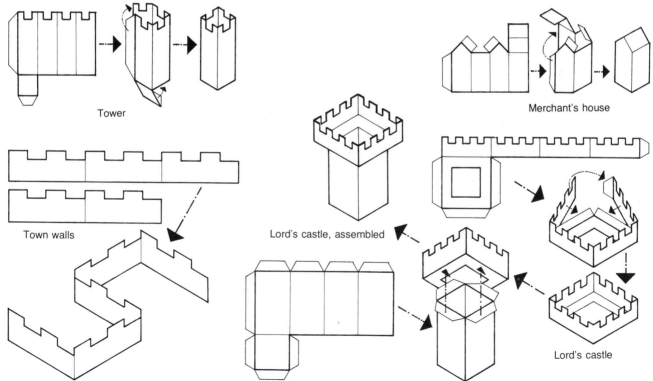

Tower

Merchant's house

Town walls

Lord's castle, assembled

Lord's castle

Players

Any number of lords and merchants can play. One player acts as banker. Each lord has one castle which occupies one square. Each merchant has eight houses representing his business establishments.

Rules

Each round of play is preceded by negotiations between the players. The lords try to induce the merchants to live in their cities. After the merchants have decided on their locations, the lords decide on their moves.

The players throw the dice for each round of play. The highest number makes the first move, the next highest follows, and so on down the line.

If a player's move results in a battle, the battle is decided by the dice but it is part of that player's move. If the person he battles with has not made his move, he can do so after the battle.

After all players have played, soldiers and merchants are paid, merchants pay their taxes to the lord, and collect profits for their businesses.

The next round of play begins with a period of negotiation, lords annex land, merchants move; the dice are thrown for the sequence of play for the following round.

1. The lords own the land or can take possession of it. They offer the merchants space inside their cities. The merchants negotiate and must pay for protection, if they decide to live in a city.

2. The more merchants a lord has within his city, the more money he can accumulate to pay soldiers.

3. The lord's power rests on his soldiers. He must pay one gold piece to each soldier after each round of play. He can have as many soldiers as he thinks he can afford.

4. The merchants can choose their towns or can operate outside of the town gates and not pay the lord.

5. A rival lord can send soldiers to overpower unprotected merchants and confiscate their money.

6. If the merchants are threatened, they can petition the lord of a town to let them inside. He can do so at a charge or leave them to be attacked by the rival lord. He can also send soldiers to fight off his rivals. He cannot attack merchants outside his own gates.

7. If the townspeople within a town become numerous enough, they can contest with the lord for possession of the town. If they can overcome his soldiers, they can eject him from the town and not pay the lord's taxes. They cannot fight lords outside of their town and can only annex land to make their town larger.

8. If the merchants outside the town gates are robbed by a rival lord, they can borrow money from other merchants to start new businesses again. If they cannot borrow money, they are out of the game.

9. Battles between lords or between lords and merchants are decided by the odds of the dice as they were in the previous games.

10. Odds of soldiers against soldiers in the open are matched. The lord with the most soldiers has the best odds. Each soldier counts as one point.

11. A lord attacking a fortified place must have three soldiers to the protected lord's two to make the odds even.

12. Townsmen attacking a lord in the open must have two townsmen to one of the lord's soldiers to even the odds. For example, they can attack him before he gets back to his castle after he has gone on a raiding party.

13. If the lord is in a tower or castle, there must be three townsmen to one of the lord's soldiers.

14. Each lord begins the game with ten soldiers and one square upon which his castle is situated. He can buy any number of soldiers if he can afford them after the first round of play.

15. Each merchant player has eight merchants. Four to seven merchants occupy one square. For over seven merchants there must be two squares.

16. As cities grow larger, the lord can take more land. He can put towers on free land and garrison them with soldiers. If there is no tower on land, the lord can take it.

17. The lord can attack the castles or towers of other lords and take their land if he cannot find free land around his town. If he takes a town, the merchants must pay taxes to him for the next round of play. They can then move to another town if they so desire.

18. The game continues until one player owns all the land on the board.

19. Towers or castles can house as many soldiers as the lord wishes to place inside of them. The other lords do not know how many soldiers are in the tower because the lord disposes of his soldiers secretly.

20. Townspeople can decide to fight on the side of their lord if they choose. If he offers to lower their taxes, they may do so. Townsmen may defend themselves against lords but do not have to engage in battles between lords.

21. Each merchant is given three gold pieces for each merchant house he owns after each round of play. He can buy more houses for five gold pieces each from the banker.

22. If merchants become very wealthy, they can buy a square from a lord and occupy it themselves without paying taxes. But they will have to defend it themselves against attacking lords.

23. Townsmen within a town, fighting against soldiers outside, have the odds of two townsmen to one of the lord's soldiers.

24. If a lord besieges a town or goes away to battle, he must leave a garrison behind. The townspeople can attack the garrison and, if they win, they can hold the town against the lord when he comes back.

25. If the lord loses a battle with the townspeople or with another lord, he is out of the game.

26. Soldiers are bought from a bank; profits from businesses are paid from the bank. The banker is one of the players. He does not gain from being banker.

The Medieval Town In America

New England was colonized by people who had definite ideas of how God should be worshipped, how to govern themselves, what industry was, and who should be master and who should be servant. These ideas were evolved in the medieval towns of England and their surrounding villages.

The New England town was built by people who had learned to work together without the domination of the nobility. The colonists built their towns on the medieval model but administered them themselves. The towns were like plants transplanted from a meager to a rich soil. They sprouted and grew healthy as soon as their roots dug into the freedom of the new world.

For a short time after their arrival, the colonists lived in much the same way as they had in England. But conditions in North America were quite different. In Europe, land had been scarce and only very important people had very much of it. In America, land was free for the taking. Europe was starved for wood; in the New World trees were so abundant that forests were chopped down to clear the land for farming. In Europe work was scarce; in America there was a shortage of skilled and unskilled labor. A North American's trade was more valuable than an Englishman's royal title.

Under these conditions, servants were no longer content to serve and the great lords found that they must look after themselves. The different conditions of the New World forced the early colonists to change their ideas of how they should build buildings and towns, of how they should own land, and how they should govern themselves. The result was that they invented new tools to build new houses and new towns to put them in.

People with strong ideas usually make them into rules. There are the gentle rules that everyone accepts, called customs, and there are the hard rules that people must obey whether they want to or not, which are called laws. People build their buildings and shape their towns to conform to these two kinds of rules.

A FAMILY OF HOUSES

The planning of New England towns was not accidental. The town's boundaries, which might be four or more miles square, were set by the General Court of the colonies. Land was granted to prospective settlers under the condition that, within a stated period of perhaps two years, they would erect houses and make a town.

The original charter-holders had the privilege of granting lands to any person willing to build his dwelling within the town boundaries and obey the town laws. The town founders were responsible for the allocation of the land. They were also bound to help the poor members of the community build their houses. If the founders did not organize a town within the stated time limit, the grant was taken from them.

Land was awarded according to family need. A married man and his family might receive twelve acres while a bachelor would be awarded only eight. The largest plot of land went to the minister and the best house in town was erected for him. Lands outside the village, such as meadowland, upland marsh, and woodlots, were also equitably divided. Controls were placed on the transfer of land and on its inheritance. As a consequence, large estates did not develop. New England became a land of small land parcels and small villages. Settlements were compact and very different from the great landed estates of the Dutch along the Hudson, the trade city of New Amsterdam, or the lordly plantations of Virginia and Maryland.

Village plans were as varied as the land they grew on. Yet they were also quite similar since they were formed by the same laws and customs. At the center of the village was the meetinghouse and the fenced-in commons with houses clustered around it. In regions near the frontier, the town was surrounded by a stockade. In more established towns the houses extended beyond the village along the highroad to the next town.

The New England town was much like a private club with a controlled membership. Admittance, although restricted, was freely granted. The practice of working for a stated period of time to pay for the passage from England, or working to pay one's debts, was quite common. When people had completed their allotted work time, they often became landowning settlers themselves. In Plymouth colony it was common practice to grant 25 acres of unmanured land to those whose terms of servitude had expired.

Houses were kept close together. The towns made laws to see that settlements did not get out of bounds. The state of Massachusetts enforced a law forbidding anyone from living more than half a mile from the meetinghouse. In Plymouth colony several men who chose to dwell in isolated houses were taken to court and fined.

New England Town Puzzle

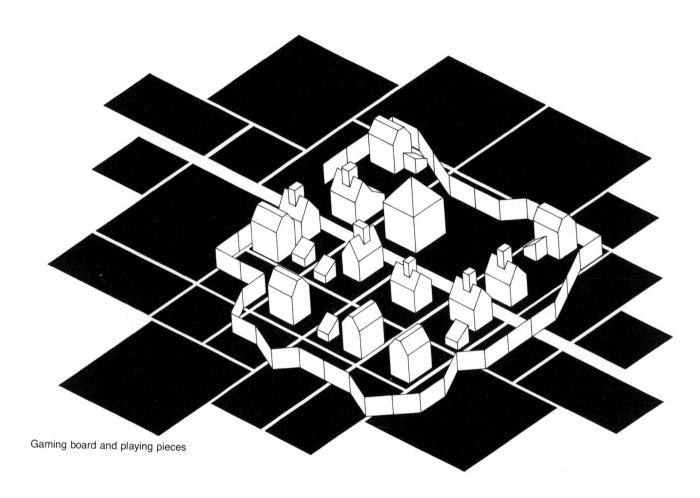

Gaming board and playing pieces

Unlike the medieval city, the New England town did not have enemies within and without. The colonists' problem was to design their village in such a way that they would be protected against the Indians whose land they were invading, but not have the protective walls interfere too much with their normal life.

The puzzle has to do with the town's geometry — that is, the arrangement of the town's parts into a pattern for survival. The rules for arranging the town are derived from the dangers of the frontier and the living patterns of the townspeople.

Materials

Select a light cardboard and cut out the land squares, houses, barns, outhouses, minister's house, meetinghouse, and fences. Glue them together as you have the other models. You can make them any size as long as they fit on the squares as shown on the drawing.

The land pieces and houses should have different colors. They can be any size as long as they are cut to the same scale as the fences.

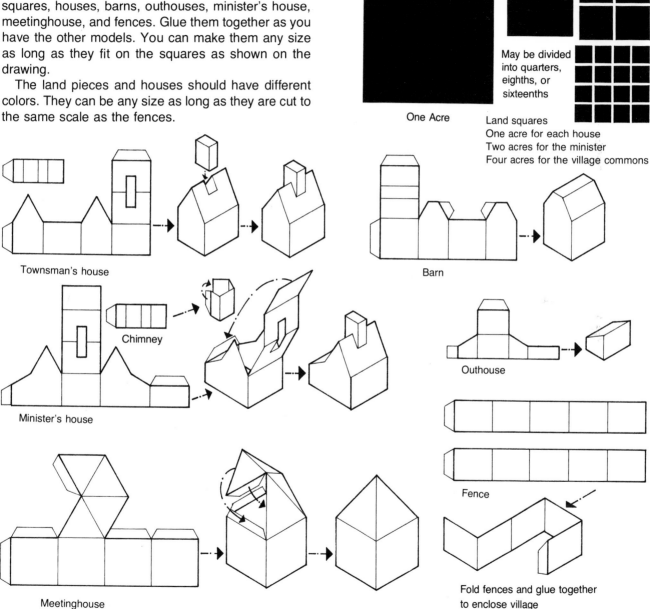

One Acre

May be divided into quarters, eighths, or sixteenths

Land squares
One acre for each house
Two acres for the minister
Four acres for the village commons

Townsman's house

Barn

Chimney

Minister's house

Outhouse

Fence

Meetinghouse

Fold fences and glue together to enclose village

Meetinghouse (about 1725)

The land is represented by various-sized pieces of paper as shown on the drawings. The largest is a full acre. There are also one-quarter and one-eighth acre pieces, as shown. An acre is really 44,000 square feet but for this game we will consider it to be 40,000 square feet, since it allows us to cut up our squares evenly.

Players

The players are the townspeople. Any number of people can play. Each townsman gets one acre of land, a house, a barn, and an outhouse. Each player also gets five pieces of fence consisting of five sections. Each fence section is about the length of a quarter acre.

The players have to enclose the minister's house and the meetinghouse as well as their own houses and buildings.

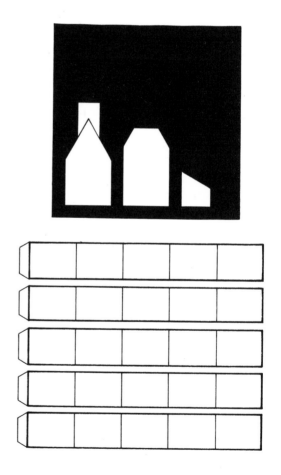

Rules

All townsmen must live within a half mile of the meetinghouse. This means that houses must be built closely together. No townsman can go through another's yard to get to his house, the meetinghouse, or the commons. We will, therefore, need roads, which will be about half the size of the 50-foot squares, or 25 feet in width.

The houses must also be kept clustered closely together for it may be necessary to enclose them with a palisade. The closer they are, the shorter the length of the palisade that surrounds them and the easier they will be to defend.

Yet there must be enough land surrounding each house — approximately one acre. If the palisade could enclose the barns and the outhouses as well, it would protect the tools, cattle, and gardens of the settlers. If it cannot, the possessions of the colonists will be lost in Indian attacks. All of the cattle can be driven together on the commons, if it can be enclosed.

A compromise must be found. If the settlers lived in a fort, they would be safe, but it would be impossible for all the people and animals to live crowded together for any length of time. On the other hand, if the palisade were large enough to enclose all of the land and or-

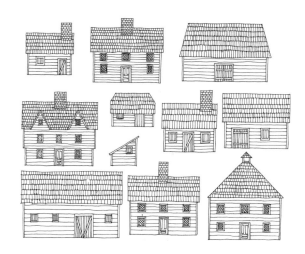

chards, they would be the most comfortable but they could not defend it easily. Somewhere, between a tight circle and a long palisade, there is a compromise which will accomplish both purposes. The squares of land, houses, roads, and commons must be arranged in such a way that the colonists can live in comfort and also be safe.

The road is very important for it is used for many purposes. If there is more than one road, there will have to be a number of gates, which are the weakest part of the palisade defense.

A mile is a little over 5,000 feet — which is only about 2,500 feet in any one direction if one is to live no further than half a mile from the meetinghouse. This would mean a town of only 20 families if the lots are all 250 feet wide in a straight line. But a good-sized town must have 100 families or more. The problem is to design the town in such a way that there will be houses in all directions around the meetinghouse so that the greatest number of people can live in the town and yet be within half a mile of the center. The town must be easy to defend and the road must take people into its center and out again by the shortest possible route.

Townsman's house

The Industrial City

Houses and factories crowded together during the middle of the
nineteenth century.

While the colonists in North America were forging a new life, the towns of England were being reformed by the industrial revolution. The industrial revolution destroyed the feudal relationship between lord and serf and with it the medieval town.

A decisive change was brought about by the increase in population. For the first time in centuries, the death rate declined below the birth rate. From the middle of the eighteenth century, England's population began to increase rapidly. According to some estimates at the beginning of the century, there were five and a half million people in England and Wales; half a century later this number had grown to seven million. At the beginning of the nineteenth century the population was nine million; thirty years later it rose to fourteen million.

The death rate had been high during the first part of the eighteenth century because of famine and alcoholism. It fell with the introduction of root crops which aided cattle raising so that the supply of fresh meat became available all year round. Beer was substituted for gin and wheat became a common cereal. More vegetables were consumed and personal cleanliness improved. Refuse dumps and graveyards were located away from the centers of population and better drainage and more fresh water were supplied to the towns.

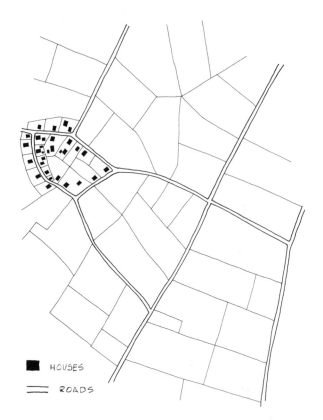

■ HOUSES

═ ROADS

Plan of an English farming village, about 1800.

With improvements in living conditions, important changes occurred in agriculture and manufacture. The "open field" system which had survived from feudalism disappeared. Land was better utilized. But the improvement of agricultural methods brought with it a worsening of the condition of the small farmer. Many were forced off their land and became tenants and laborers.

The uprooted population turned to industrial work — particularly in the weaving industry. Weaving had formerly been a cottage industry, conducted in the worker's home. The process of spinning, weaving, and dyeing was carried on by the same family that bought raw wool and sold finished cloth.

New machines, such as the spinning jenny, were invented which enabled one worker to produce many more garments. The jenny and the fly shuttle were first used in country dwellings, but the quantity of the yarn and cloth produced by each machine was limited to the energy that could be exerted by physical labor alone.

During the last part of the eighteenth century, the first water-driven spinning machines were invented. Shortly afterwards, the steam engine replaced water power. The weaving industry abandoned its scattered, cottage-industry operation and concentrated in large workshops where water or steam energy was available. At first, these factories were sited near watercourses but later, as steam replaced water power, they were relocated near coal mines. The establishment of these factories was the basis upon which the first mill towns — such as Manchester, England — grew into industrial cities.

The steam engine solved the problem of water seepage in the mines and revolutionized mining techniques. Coal improved the potential of the steam engine and wood was abandoned as a fuel.

At the same time, coke was substituted for charcoal in the smelting of iron ore. A method was then discovered to utilize coal in the forging and rolling of iron. This put the iron industry in a position to supply the newly mechanized weaving industry with iron machinery. Foundries, blast furnaces, and weaving mills moved from wooded regions to coal mining areas. The result was the growth of large, self-contained manufacturing operations.

The rapidly expanding cotton manufacturing industry of Lancashire depended on raw material bought from other lands. As a result of the need for raw cotton, the manufacture of cotton goods was closely connected with the slave trade. Although the slave trade was shared by the French, the Dutch, and the Portuguese, more than half the slaves carried across the Atlantic to the New World made the passage in the holds of English ships.

In 1771 alone it is estimated that fifty thousand slaves were transported from Africa to the New World. The trip from Africa to the West Indies or North America was called the "middle passage," for it was only part of the slave ships' journey. The slavers carried cargos of finished woven cotton goods to Africa, exchanged them for Negroes, took the slaves across the Atlantic to the West Indies or the southern United States, and exchanged them for cargos of raw cotton, tobacco, and sugar, which they then brought back to England.

The planters of the West Indies and the American mainland bought slaves and Lancashire cotton goods to clothe them. The supply of Negro labor from Africa enabled the colonies to provide the raw cotton for the English weaving industry. The slave trade and the manufacture of cotton goods were thus inextricably entwined.

In the last forty years of the eighteenth century a degree of technical progress was achieved which made possible an unlimited increase in industrial production. The development of industries and their concentration in large factories drew many families from the agricultural and mining districts. They came from isolated country dwellings to live in cramped hovels surrounding the factories. New towns were born while old ones grew out of all proportion to their original plans or capacities for housing the expanded population.

The changes caused the majority of England's population to alter both their place of residence and their way of life. It revolutionized the use of land and modified the appearance of the countryside. The result of industrialization was an overwhelming increase in town dwellings, along with new roads and canals. Towns were born and doubled their size within a generation.

Factories, roads, and canals were built with startling swiftness. Mines were opened in the heart of the agricultural countryside. Blast furnaces and factory chimneys rose to the sky alongside of cathedral spires.

Houses in the town were built near the place of work. Factory smoke permeated the houses and factory waste polluted the water. Industrial movement was hopelessly impeded by private traffic. The chaos was aggravated by the factories which constantly transformed and expanded. Houses were demolished and rebuilt, as the outskirts of the cities crept further into the countryside.

Manchester was a village of twelve thousand inhabitants in the middle of the eighteenth century, but by the beginning of the nineteenth century it had grown to a town of ninety-five thousand and by the middle of the same century the population was over four times as great.

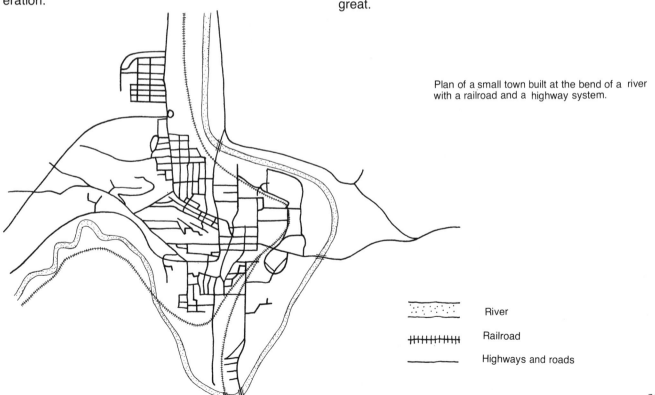

Plan of a small town built at the bend of a river with a railroad and a highway system.

.... River

╫╫╫╫╫╫ Railroad

———— Highways and roads

The Game of Industrialization

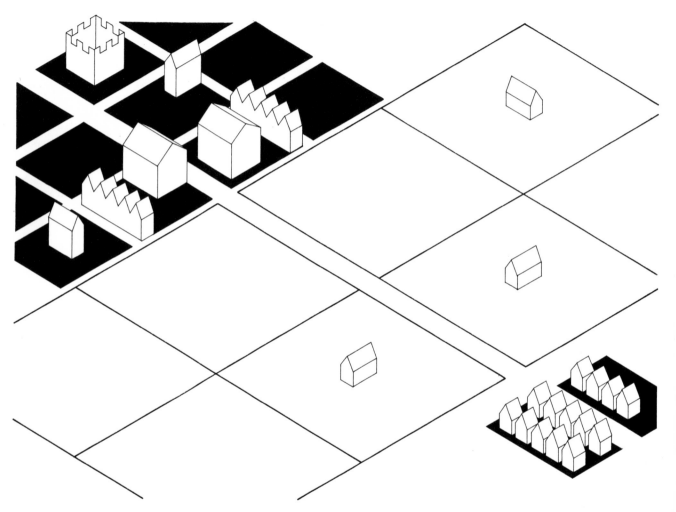

Gaming board and playing pieces

This is a contest between the city factory owners and the country landowners; the setting is during the industrial revolution in England at the beginning of the nineteenth century.

Materials

A map of town and country (see drawing). It depicts the land in the village, the road to the city, and the city with factories and a poorhouse. Markers represent labor mills, farmhouses, and the village. A pair of dice is required to indicate the numbers of varying conditions affecting the squire and millowners which then affect the laborers and farmers. Several packets of play money are also required.

Players

The game is played by four groups of players — the country squire who owns and rents the land; farmers who rent land; the city millowners; and the laborers, who may work on the country land or in the city factories. Any player can be the banker, although it is suggested that this task be performed by the squire. The banker does not receive any compensation for his services.

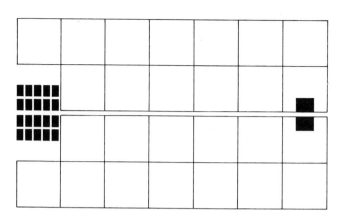

Markers for workers
Fold and cut markers as required

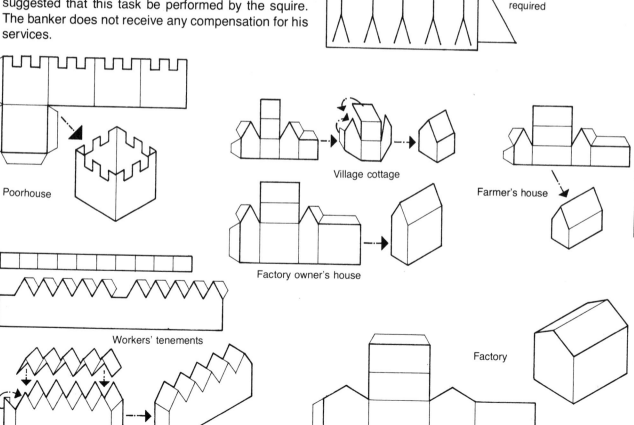

Poorhouse

Village cottage

Factory owner's house

Farmer's house

Workers' tenements

Factory

Rules

1. The landowner owns the land surrounding the village and town, and rents land to farmers who hire laborers to help work the land.

2. The productivity of the land is a function of the labor invested in it. Each plot of land must be worked by 10 workers for maximum productivity. Its productivity is reduced by 10 percent for every worker short of this number. After each plot of land has 10 workers, another plot of land must be rented for additional productivity.

3. Land is rented from the squire and payment made to the banker. Then negotiations are made with laborers to work the land.

4. The millowners also need laborers to run their mills and must offer high wages to the farm laborers to attract them away from the land to the city.

5. The millowners purchase factory pieces, hire laborers, and place them in the factory squares to produce goods for the market. Each mill can hire 10 workers. Workers must work in lots of 10. If there is one worker less, productivity is reduced by 10 percent. For more than 10 workers, another mill must be purchased.

6. Factory space must be rented from the banker.

7. The dice are thrown for numbers corresponding to the fluctuation of the market and the demand for goods.

8. For each round of play all players must pay subsistence to the banker, in proportion to their style of life. Millowners, for example, must maintain an establishment costing several times that of the laborers. The farmers pay more than the laborers but less than the millowners.

9. Any player who cannot pay his subsistence must go to the poorhouse.

10. The maintenance of the poorhouse is paid by the millowners in proportion to the numbers of mills they own.

11. All players begin with resources. The squire has land squares which he rents to the farmers. The laborers have small savings. The millowners have capital with which they rent factory land and buy machinery.

12. If the mills shut down for lack of work, the laborers must have enough money to return to their village where they can live until there is another demand for their labor.

13. The laborers may band together and rent land from the squire and become landowners themselves, or they may acquire mill machinery and become millowners. In this instance they form a cooperative and all share equally in the profits.

14. The farmers may be forced to return to the village.

15. Players representing laborers have 20 laborers each. A laborer can decide to work in the mill, or on the land, or in both places. His objective is to earn as much in wages as possible.

16. A mill must have 10 laborers to operate to full capacity. For over 10 laborers, a new mill has to be bought. For under 10 laborers, payment is according to the number of workers in the mill.

17. City land costs 10 credit points in rent for each round of play.

18. Farmland costs 2 credit points per round of play.

19. Mills earn 4 credit points per worker in an average round of play. This will vary according to how the dice indicate various conditions.

20. Farmland earns 3 credit points per worker depending on the play. It can be more or less.

21. Villagers working on the land do not pay rent; they live in the village.

22. City workers pay 1 credit point per worker for rent.

23. If a worker goes to the poorhouse, the millowner has to pay 1 credit point per worker in the poorhouse.

24. If a worker goes to the poorhouse, he has to work for the millowner when the millowner wants to hire him. He must stay in the poorhouse until the millowner will let him out. He cannot return to the village.

25. Travel back to the village costs 2 credit points.

26. The millowner has 50 credit points at the beginning of the game.

27. The squire does not have credit points, he has land.

28. Farmers who hire laborers have 50 credit points.

29. Workers have 5 credit points each at the beginning of the game.

30. If the city gets larger, that is, there is more need for city land, the squire can rent land to the millowners at city rates. He subdivides it and rents it at 10 units a plot.

31. The plan can be made larger or smaller according to the number of players.

32. Each plot of city land will hold one factory and housing for 20 workers.

33. The millowner pays 4 credit points rent on his house in the city. It has a separate block of its own.

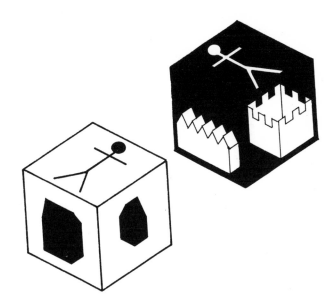

The objective of the game is for each playing group to maximize its wealth. If the millowners offer higher wages than the farmers, the laborers may move to the city to work in the mills. The production of the mills is a function of the laborers working in them, as is the productivity of the land. However, a mill can only employ a certain number of laborers. If the millowner wishes to employ more, he must buy more mill machinery. Production is increased from one mill to a several-mill machine factory. The millowner may also have to rent more land to increase the size of his mill.

The millowner anticipates continued demand for his products and gambles that the market will increase.

The laborers try to get as high wages as they can. They will, therefore, attempt to force the farm owners and the millowners to compete for their wages. They may refuse to work and may live on their savings until the farmers or millowners accept their demands.

The farmer and the millowner will each try to pay his laborers as little as possible to maximize his profits. However, if wages are too low, the workers will be forced into the poorhouse, which the millowner must support.

Game Card *(Fluctuations of the market — see the 21 dice combinations on page 30)*

1-1 — An increased demand for cotton clothing for the slaves in North America increases the demand on the mills. The millowners can double their production capacity. Factories pay their owners double.

1-2 — A normal year. The mills sell all of their production and the farmers market their crops.

1-3 — An increased demand for uniforms and food for the soldiers fighting Napoleon means that there is a tripling of the market. Factories pay their owners triple.

1-4 — A bad year for crops. The land produces only one-half of a production unit for each area under cultivation. Mill production is normal.

1-5 — A normal year. All units pay.

1-6 — A defeat of the English armies. Taxes are raised. Landowners must pay one-quarter of their profits, millowners must pay one-half and laborers one-tenth. It is a normal productive year otherwise.

2-2 — The market has been overloaded. The factory owners cannot sell their goods. They must either lay off workers or pay them while they stand idle. Land productivity is normal.

2-3 — A slave revolt in North America. The millowners cannot get material for their mills. They must lay off workers or absorb the cost of their maintenance.

2-4 — A fire in the mills. Each millowner loses half of his productive capacity.

2-5 — A normal year.

2-6 — Cotton production is increased in the British West Indies. More slaves are needed. The millowners can increase their production by half. Factories pay their owners 50 percent over a normal year.

3-3 — A bumper year. All the land pays double. The millowners have a normal productive year.

3-4 — A bumper crop for the farmers — all land units pay double. Normal year for the millowners.

3-5 — A depression occurs. No one will buy either cotton goods or food. There is no money. The millowners lose half of their production by selling it at lower cost. Half of the food production is allowed to rot on the ground because it cannot be sold.

3-6 — More slaves are introduced into North America. Demand for cotton goods again increases one-half. Factories pay their owners 50 percent over a normal year.

4-4 — A normal year.

4-5 — A normal year.

4-6 — A normal year.

5-5 — Production increases through use of new machinery but the market does not. Half of the laborers can be laid off with production staying at normal levels.

5-6 — A shortage of coal decreases cotton production by one-half. Food production remains the same.

6-6 — A normal year.

The Cattle Town

At the end of the Civil War, the South was very poor and the North was starved for lack of meat. The Texans began driving their herds of Longhorn cattle northward to the railroad terminals to ship them off to the meat-packing plants of the large northern cities.

For a short period of time immediately following the Civil War, towns were born and grew to maturity in the space of a decade.

The cattle town was simply a market facility situated at the junction of the railroad and the Texas cattle trail.

An entrepreneur would hire a surveyor, lay out a neat grid of blocks and streets, and the town was started. The owner would file a plot with the county register of deeds and begin sellings lots. A few months later the town would have attracted the first business elements of a settlement — a general store, a blacksmith shop, a post office, and a saloon with rooms above that doubled as a hotel. The railroad would lay tracks to the town and the Texas cattlemen would drive their herds to the rail terminal.

A large stockyard would be built, a barn, an office, and a set of livestock scales installed. Shortly thereafter, as the cattle trade prospered, an elegant hotel and livery stable would also appear in the town. A bank might follow these basic amenities. The railroad, for its part, would install a freight office, a telegraph line, and a crew of agents and clerks to process cattle shipments.

The residents of the town came there to get rich as quickly as they could. The center of the community's economic base was the cattleman, who drove his cattle to the railhead year after year. The attraction of the trade was simply the difference between the value of cattle on their native prairies and what the northern cattle buyers would pay for them at the city meat-packing centers.

Livestock buyers congregated each season at the cattle towns. Some were simply cattle speculators. Others represented groups of purchasers, such as buyers for the ranchers of Colorado, the Dakotas,

Wyoming, and Montana. There was a demand in these territories for yearlings and two-year-olds as stock cattle. Driving cattle from the market town northwestward became quite as common as driving them from Texas to the market town.

Feeders of the Middle West also bought full-grown steers for final fattening and representatives of the packinghouses of the eastern markets were in the cattle town to buy beef for slaughter.

In the very beginning some of the drovers made spectacular profits but at best it was a risky business. The cattle drover could decline to sell to cattle-town buyers and could instead choose to ship his own beef to a terminal market for sale — or a livestock commission merchant would do this for him. This involved a gamble on the part of the drover. The terminal markets promised greater profits. The operation involved heavy freight charges and there was always the risk of a sudden market plunge between the time the cattle were loaded and the time they reached their destination.

For the cattleman, the losses could be appalling. In a year of poor cattle demand he courted the sudden catastrophe of shipping to a terminal and watching the prices fall even lower or suffering the slow agony of awaiting a local price upturn.

The economic lifeblood of the town was not the cattle trade itself, but the enterprises that serviced the personnel of the cattle trade. For the local businessman, the appeal of the cattle business was the need for consumer goods and services. He cheerfully provided all the drover's wants from harnesses to dance-hall girls.

The cattle trade was of great importance to the railroad, for the western livestock filled the critical need for eastbound freight. Without the cattle trade the trains would return from the frontier empty.

Originally, the cattlemen were only occasional visitors to the town, arriving in the spring and leaving in the late fall. The cattle town might be virtually vacant from December through April. When the southern ranchers began ranching nearby, or on the borders of the state, the life of the town changed. Cattle drives were shorter and were made several times during the year rather than in one large seasonal drive. This meant that cattlemen spent more time in the towns. Cowboys and ranchers from relatively nearby holdings became frequent town visitors. However, the periodic influxes of cattle and cattlemen from the Texas Panhandle continued regularly throughout this period and autumn remained the favored shipping time for the ranchers.

The cattle drives began to stimulate other businesses. Livestock that was not sold at the railhead was often bought by local speculators. These cattle would be turned loose to forage for themselves. Those that survived the winter emerged thin and gaunt in the spring but they were readily fattened on the new prairie grasses in time for the early summer sales. These animals were more marketable than the gaunt Longhorns just off the trail. In addition, they no longer carried the splenic fever which was the bane of Texas cattle.

The winter speculation in cattle grew into a major business for some townsmen and some Texas ranchers moved north, closer to the town, and bought houses in town to enjoy its social amenities.

At first, farming was discouraged by the townspeople. The cattle herds ate the crops, broke the fences, and damaged the farmer's crops. The Texans refused to tend their cattle, and bloodshed was often narrowly averted. When the drovers were taken into court as the result of these trespasses, the courts of the townspeople favored the drovers since business depended upon the cattle trade.

But farming raised real estate values. Land costs increased in proximity to the nearest town. There was an intrinsic conflict — the townspeople made their living from the cattle drovers but district court prosecutions were financed by the county at large. The farmers had to share in the expenses of the cattle-town felonies. The rural taxpayers objected to bearing the financial burden of an abnormal crime rate caused by the cattle trade. The public funds voted by the town for general improvement usually went toward accommodating and encouraging the cattle trade instead of farming.

A bare decade after the cattle towns had begun, their end was near. Homesteaders began to crowd onto the grazing lands. The great majority of dirt farmers came in wagons bringing their families, cattle, horses, farming implements, and household furniture. The town could not service the conflicting interests of both the farmers and the ranchers.

Each of the cattle towns felt the force of these two utterly irreconcilable economic interests. Each town, one after another, at the expense of the commerce in range cattle, submitted to the steadying influence of the farmer.

Rural settlement began to take place on a large scale on the land surrounding the towns. The farmers overflowed onto the hitherto empty grazing ground upon which the Texas drover depended to sustain his cattle.

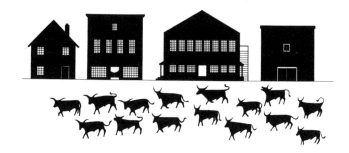

Real estate entrepreneurs and speculators exploited the sale of the land around the town with the same gusto as when they lured the drovers to the towns to sell them goods. The speculators opened land offices, divided their lands into lots and streets, and sold them as housing lots and farm sites.

Barbed wire had not yet come onto the market. The costs of enclosing farmland was therefore prohibitive. It was necessary to pass laws against herds and quarantine laws against the Texas splenic fever to protect the farmer's crops and cattle. Since the Texas drovers would surely be the most persistent offenders, the ideal expedient was to close the country to the cattle trade.

The herds of cattle that had been lured to the cattle towns to prosper the townspeople were now considered as retarding the development of the country by deterring its settlement and cultivation.

As might be expected, the real estate entrepreneurs were the most active advocates for herd and quarantine laws. One by one the towns passed herd laws as the land surrounding them filled up with farmers. The railroads finally passed south into Texas itself while the agricultural settlements surrounded the towns and choked off the cattle trail.

The Cattle Town Game

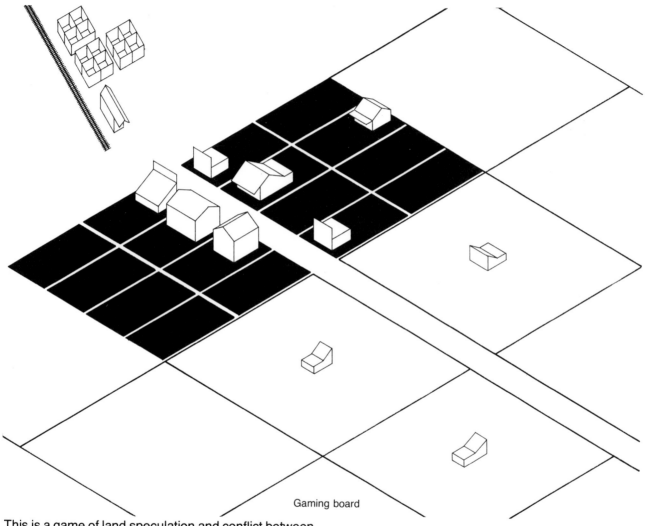

Gaming board

This is a game of land speculation and conflict between the cattle drover and the farmer. The cattlemen want free access to the town across the farmers' land. The farmers want to protect their crops. The townspeople will favor whichever of the two conflicting forces will benefit them the most.

69

Materials

Five dice, cutouts as shown, paper money, and a map as shown in the drawing.

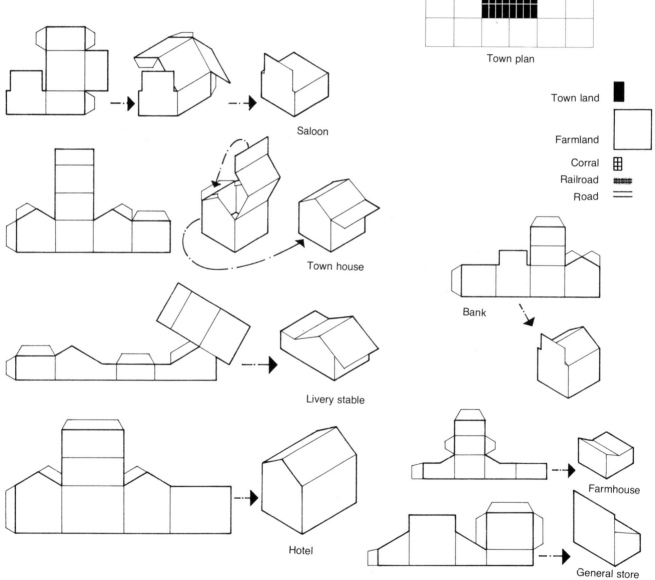

Town plan

Town land

Farmland

Corral

Railroad

Road

Saloon

Town house

Livery stable

Bank

Hotel

Farmhouse

General store

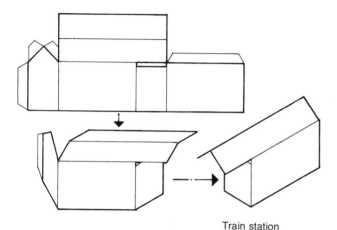

Train station

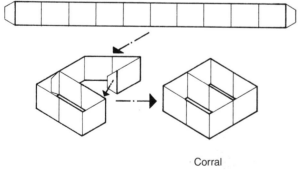

Corral

Cattle

Players

Players consist of a cattle agent, store keepers, ranchers, farmers (homesteaders), a banker, and an entrepreneur.

Rules

1. The entrepreneur owns the town land.

2. Homesteaders can homestead land around the town. The entrepreneur cannot buy and sell this land unless he gains possession from a homesteader.

3. Only homesteaders can sell the land they homestead.

4. There is one cattle drive a year.

5. The cattlemen have $20,000. They buy cattle in Texas and bring them to the cattle town. They must pay $8. a head in Texas. This price is fixed. They may sell them for any price they can get in the cattle town. Money for the cattle should be paid into a kitty. No one gets this money. Texas ranchers are not in the game.

6. When the cattleman gets to the cattle town, he can gamble with the cattle agent to sell his cattle or sell them to the townspeople. If he gambles with the cattle agent, they determine the price that will be paid with the poker dice. The highest hand wins. If the cattleman's price is too high, the cattle agent will not gamble; if the cattle agent's price is too low, the cattleman will not gamble.

If the cattleman cannot gamble with the cattle agent or sell to the townspeople, he can ship the cattle himself. He must pay $2. a head to ship them, and he throws the dice to see the price he will receive on the eastern market. To find this price, the cattleman takes four dice and throws them once. The total number of points on the four dice represents the price he will be paid by the banker for each head of cattle.

The cattle agent is paid $2. per head for all cattle shipped, no matter how much or how little he pays for them.

7. The cattleman must return to Texas to buy more cattle for the next drive.

8. All cattle must come from Texas. Once they are sold in the cattle town the only way of getting more cattle is to return to Texas and take the chance of the cattle drive.

9. If homesteaders buy the cattle, they must pay $2. a head to feed them for a year, then sell them to the cattle agent or ship, taking the same chances that the cattleman does.

10. The stores are of three kinds: those that sell predominantly to the cattleman, those that sell to the farmers, and those that sell about equally to both. The hotel and bar owner sell to the cattlemen. The general store sells more to farmers than to cattlemen. The blacksmith shop sells to both.

11. Each store makes the profit indicated. If crops are good, the general store prospers; if the cattle drive is good, the saloon and hotel prospers. The storekeepers gamble with either the homesteaders or cattlemen.

12. Each player, except for the entrepreneur, starts with money. Instead of money, the entrepreneur has the land plots shown. The banker has the bank. He has $20,000. He must pay $10,000. for the bank.

13. Each storekeeper has $5,000; the general store costs $2,500; the hotel costs $2,500; saloons cost $2,000. each; the blacksmith shop costs $1,000.

14. A house to place on a house lot in town costs $1,000. House lots cost whatever the entrepreneur can get. He also sells town lots for whatever he can get. Homesteads are 50 acres. The squares indicate homestead lots. Each year the homesteader earns $500. on his land. He pays $100. at the general store and $50. at the blacksmith shop.

15. The cattleman pays half of his profits in the town. 5 percent goes to the general store, 25 percent to the saloon, 15 percent to the blacksmith shop, and 5 percent to the hotel.

16. The cattle agent earns 10 percent of all the cattle he ships. He can invest this money in the town, in cattle, in banking, or in farming.

17. The storekeepers borrow from the bank, the cattlemen borrow from the bank, as do the homesteaders if they want to go into business. The banker charges interest. If the player cannot pay, the bank forecloses and takes the business — but it cannot take the land. If the homesteader cannot pay his debts, he must sell his land to the entrepreneur and pay back the bank with the money. When a player goes broke, he is out of business.

18. If a player makes a lot of money, he can go into the banking business and compete with the bank to lend money.

19. Store pieces must be bought and land within the town must be bought from the entrepreneur. Only city land can have stores. Homestead land can be used only for farming or for cattle raising.

20. If the homesteader or the rancher makes enough money, he can buy land in town and move into town. He can then vote in the town elections.

21. Neither the homesteader nor the rancher can vote. The townsmen vote on the herd laws. These benefit only the homesteaders and the businesses that deal with them.

22. The entrepreneur can extend the town by buying homestead land next to the town site and turning it into building lots.

23. The land closest to the town is therefore more valuable. When the homesteaders start they throw dice to see what homestead land they will take.

24. Anyone can change their business as they care to.

25. Each cow represents 100 cattle. Cattle are bought and sold in lots of 100.

26. A homestead plot will only support 100 cattle. If more are to be raised, more land must be obtained.

27. The game begins with the plots shown. More land can be added to the game but it has to go through homesteaders.

28. Each year, when the cattlemen bring their cattle into town, each farmer is taxed one-tenth of his income to keep law and order in the town.

29. Cattlemen can drive their cattle into town any way they choose. If they drive them through the center of town, all the businesses must pay one-tenth of their earnings for the damage. If they drive them through homestead land, each homesteader along their way between the outskirts of town and the stockyards loses one-fifth of his crops for that year.

30. Cattlemen will drive through land not homesteaded if a path is free, but as the land becomes occupied they cannot get into the town without driving over someone's land.

POKER DICE

The game is played with five dice. Winning dice combinations are similar to poker hands. (See drawing below)

The first player throws the dice, selects that combination that he thinks will make the best hand and puts them aside. He then throws the remaining dice again to see if he can better his hand. For example if he has one pair he puts these aside and tries to make his hand three of a kind or better. If he has three of a kind he throws for a full house or four of a kind and so on.

After the second throw of the dice they are passed to the next player. The highest poker hand wins.

NUMBERS	CHANCES
2....1	1 + 1
3....2	2 + 1, 1 + 2
4....3	3 + 1, 2 + 2, 1 + 3
5....4	4 + 1, 3 + 2, 2 + 3, 1 +4
6....5	5 + 1, 4 + 2, 3 + 3, 2 + 4, 1 + 5
7....6	6 + 1, 5 + 2, 4 + 3, 3 + 4, 2 + 5, 1 + 6
8....5	6 + 2, 5 + 3 , 4 + 4, 3 + 5, 2 + 6
9....4	6 + 3, 5 + 4, 4 + 5, 3 + 6
10....3	6 + 4, 5 + 5, 4 +6
11....2	6 + 5, 5 + 6
12....1	6 + 6

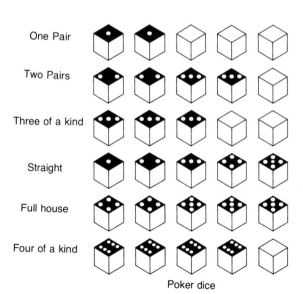

Poker dice

The Modern City

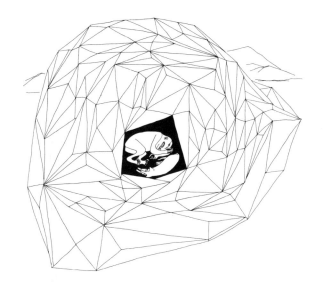

In primitive societies man's relation to his environment was a simple life and death matter. His survival depended upon the artifacts he could produce. Food protected from starvation, shelter assured survival against the extremes of temperature, and weapons protected man against predators and other men.

Survival was a nip and tuck affair, with man's brains and technology affording him a slight edge over the other animals that contested against him for survival.

In those days human activity had a no-nonsense value — there was no childhood and there were no children. Fire sustained human life and its worth could be measured by the energy it took to cut and gather firewood. The value of a wooden shelter or crude stone enclosure could be measured by the energy required to build it and its effectiveness in preserving human life.

A human life was simply equated to what a man could do. Physically defective newborn children were left to die. The old — who no longer had the vitality to produce as much food as they ate or gather fuel for the warmth they required, and who took up more space than they could build — wandered away and died. The artifacts man made were measured by how much energy it took to produce them.

Industrialization obscured this equation of man's energy to life-sustaining artifacts. As machine technology became more sophisticated, it became difficult to measure human energy against machine power. A man can measure his strength against that of a horse because both are derived from muscles. A stream's current that turns a water mill can be felt. The gears that transform water or wind power to useful work can be observed.

As power sources became more complex — from stream to steam, from electric to atomic power — goods were produced without visible human effort. When the power of two hundred horses can be contained underneath an automobile hood and activated by the slight pressure of a child's foot, the strength of man is no longer a comprehensible unit of measurable energy.

Today it is only during periods of mass technological malfunction, such as power failures, that city dwellers comprehend the human scale in relation to the amount of space and energy consumed in their environment. A building's height becomes very real when a person climbs the stairs instead of ascending in an elevator. A candle is a flicker compared to even the smallest fluorescent fixture.

It is this difference in the world around us that makes modern human settlements so difficult to comprehend. They cannot be encompassed by our senses alone. We must employ other means of understanding them. In order to comprehend the multitude of functions it is necessary to interpret data. Personal observation is no longer reliable. Mathematical equations are needed to simulate human actions, and the plans of human settlements become complex abstractions rather than perceptual notations of familiar places.

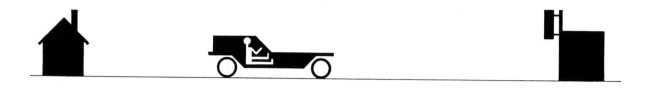

To place all of a city's functions together at once, each acting in relation to the other, involves numerous simultaneous functions. Such complex problems can only be solved by very accomplished mathematicians or by a computer.

The primary characteristic of a city is density. In planning, density means the number of people per square acre of land. The way of life of the city's people depends upon the amount of space they occupy.

When people live one or two per acre, they must have transportation to connect them to the services they require, such as food, schools, or places of business.

If there are 25 people per square acre, the separation of vehicles and people is not important. It may not even be necessary to provide sidewalks. The number of encounters between people and vehicles is small. It is also not necessary to design buildings in such a way that people need privacy from each other.

The speed of a person walking at a little over three miles an hour is incompatible with the speed of an automobile moving at 60 miles an hour. The two must be isolated from each other if the density of the settlement is such that they will meet. As density increases, the number of encounters between pedestrians and vehicles increases. At over 100 people per acre the two must be segregated.

On the other hand, low-density land occupancy cannot support shopping, restaurants, cinemas, medical centers, or schools within convenient distance of the settlement's inhabitants. In densities up to 100 people per acre, access to communal activities requires that people own automobiles. These must be used for every human activity no matter how trivial. For example, a man may require two tons of automobile to go half a mile to buy a three-ounce pack of cigarettes.

There are densities which make the problem of designing very difficult. At between 100 and 200 people per acre vehicle segregation is necessary, but the cost of walkways and bridges cannot be spread over enough people to make them feasible. A vertical segregation of people, which would be the most effective under the circumstances, requires more than 200 people per acre to be economically feasible.

Good dwellings, not excessively high, and equipped with every convenience, can be designed up to a density of 300 people per acre. The design of such dwellings, however, involves a considerable amount of skill; it must allow a reasonable amount of sunlight to reach each dwelling and provide privacy, as well as open space, for the settlement's occupants.

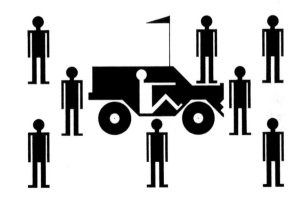

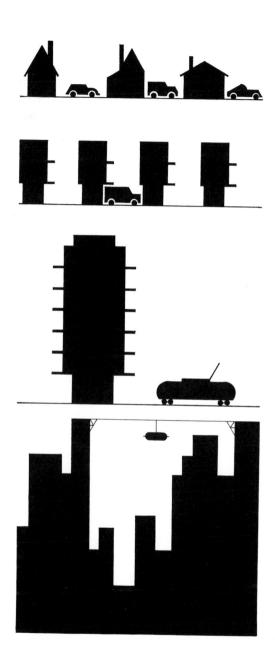

With an increase in density, pedestrian decks and bridges would permit easy personal and vehicular access to all dwellings. The increase would also support communal facilities in a minimum area of housing.

One square mile at 250 people per square acre would contain over 40,000 people. The greatest distance between any amenity and any one occupant would be the mere distance of an eight-minute walk and there could still be a great deal of public open space between the buildings.

At densities of this magnitude the motor car does not have to be used — it becomes a luxury instead of a necessity. Instead, a network of public transport can be supplied. Rapid-transit systems are only economically feasible with high densities.

At certain densities the character of the city changes. We can go from a few people per acre, where there is adequate privacy but a good deal of energy expended in acquiring goods and services, to a large number of people, where privacy is difficult to achieve but amenities are located within the range of a small amount of effort.

Convenience of city services is in inverse ratio to privacy and private space. This is the problem that occupies the architects and planners of a city. They try to devise forms that will allow visual and auditory privacy within range of the city's amenities.

But when people are closely confined, no matter how skillfully their dwellings are designed, they display symptoms of a variety of emotional disorders — higher rates of personal crime, mental instability, and other unsettling social problems. The game of planning cities of high density needs the sociologist, the psychologist, and the anthropologist among its players, as well as the architect, the planner, and the entrepreneur.

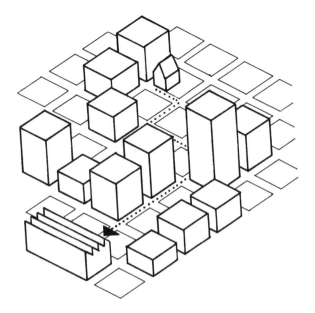

THE CITY AS A SET OF OBSTACLES

A city can be thought of as a set of obstacles in space. Each volume, such as a dwelling, office building, store, or garage, can be considered an obstacle against the free movement of the inhabitants of the city who are obliged to go around it to reach their destinations.

But one man's obstacle is another man's destination. Volumes are not only obstacles but departure points, or terminal points, for the movement of certain other of the city's inhabitants. Any possible route of any one inhabitant links a departure point to a terminal point. Any other volume that the inhabitant meets on his route is an obstacle. Every volume in a city is a departure point or a terminal point for a given number of inhabitants and an obstacle for all others.

The city, conceived as such a network, is in reality a maze of departure points and terminal points separated by obstacles. If the frequency of movements of the city's inhabitants between their departure points and target points is studied, the result will reveal the behavior pattern of the inhabitants.

From this description a complete list of possibilities can be constructed. If the number of steps between the departure point and the target can be found and these are multiplied by the frequency of their occurrence, the total will be an indication of the general effort expended in the city.

The amount of effort required to move in the city should serve as a warning device for the planner, the architect, the urbanist, and the sociologist. They could choose admissible amounts of effort for the city's inhabitants and study the problem scientifically.

In many instances this may well be too late. The energy required for the average worker in a large city to make the journey from his home to his place of work in the morning and then return in the evening would seem to have already passed permissible levels.

The human settlements of the past were a collection of houses or devices to enclose the inhabitants and protect them against climatic conditions. They were like extensions of the clothing worn — they could be heated or they could be used to keep the heat out.

Hunting tribes that roamed over great areas caused very little environmental dislocation. Their refuse soon turned back into the earth and fertilized it. The wood they burned grew again into new trees and the water they dirtied cleansed itself a few hundred yards away along the stream banks.

The house today is both an enclosure to temper the environment and a collection of mechanical devices to extend daylight, to carry away waste materials, to supply fresh water, and to control cooking fires. The house is as much a collection of terminals of the mechanical systems that allow us to live at high densities as it is an enclosure.

There is a very significant difference between the two functions. The enclosure can be built almost anywhere but the mechanical devices that terminate in the house are part of a linked system.

To be habitable at high densities, houses must have these services. At present, cities, towns, and even villages are built over a network of services buried in the earth and carried in wires overhead. It has been proposed by some architects that we recognize this network of services as a permanent, invisible part of a human settlement.

With this idea also goes another — the idea of people designing their own homes as they have for centuries. However, instead of putting his home together piece by piece, the potential home owner would be able to obtain all the component parts, thanks to industrialized housing techniques. The user of the space would then select the housing configuration he thought best for his use and either assemble it himself or have it assembled and plugged into the infrastructure of services just described. The function of the architect then changes; instead of designing individual houses, he begins to devise systems that will make it possible for the individual to exercise his housing options within the infrastructure of services.

A method of realizing this was proposed by the architect Yona Friedmann, who planned to have it installed in a computer for the world's fair in Osaka, Japan, in 1970. The prospective user would select the space he desired on a computer keyboard and then combine the spaces as he thought best. The house would be installed within the infrastructure of services at the desired position.

The computer would instantly inform the user about the design of the house and how much his unit would cost. It would tell him how far he was away from potential places of employment, how close he was to medical services, where the nearest schools would be located — in short, all of the information necessary for him to locate his dwelling place to suit his needs.

It would be assumed that the basic dwelling unit would be without decoration and that the user could clip on the cultural decoration of his choice. For example, if he wanted his house to look like a Greek temple, he could buy plastic Doric columns, possibly with neon lights inside.

Perhaps one cannot design a city, but it may be possible to help evolve the rules that determine a city's design. The rules that shape a city's design can be put into the hands of those who will live in these cities. The work of the architect and planner would be to let the people know what the rules are, how they are used, and what happens when they do not adhere to the rules.

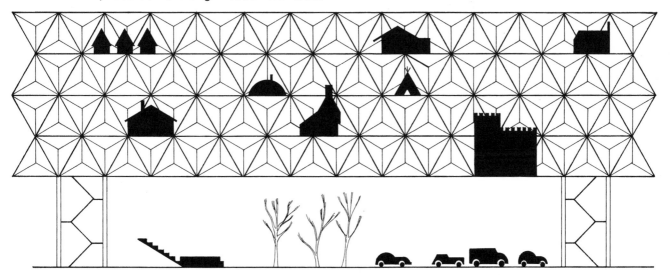

The Growth of A City Game

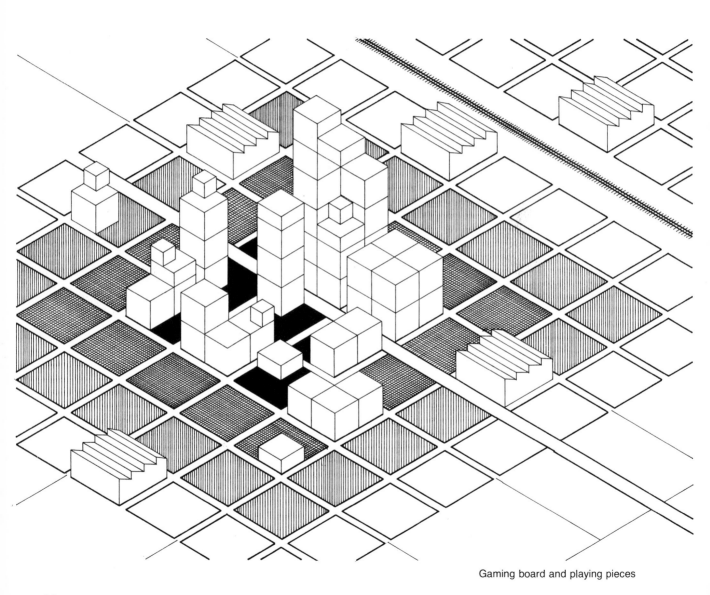

Gaming board and playing pieces

Our city begins as a river town. The river is its source of power and its means of transportation. Factories powered by water mills grow up along its banks and the factory workers cluster around them.

A little later steam engines are brought into use and with them coal for fuel. Some of the factories change their water mills for steam engines and remain on the river bank, but this is only a temporary expedient. New factories are built away from the river, where it is less crowded. These factories are more efficient because they are designed for steam engines. But they are not too far from the river for this is how their fuel is brought to them and how they ship their finished products. But soon the steam engine is applied to transportation and railroads make their appearance. Factories no longer have to be near the river but instead are built near the railroad tracks. The railroad brings fuel and raw materials for manufacture and carries away the finished products.

Living next to the factories becomes very unpleasant. The air is full of smoke, it is very noisy, and the streets are crowded and congested with factory pedestrian traffic. Those that can afford to do so move to another part of town or to the suburbs. The areas around the factories become slums. Businesses become larger and office buildings are built. Stores are established to cater to the factory workers as well as to the managers and factory owners.

The riverfront decays and falls out of use. The center of the manufacturing district is now marked by the railroad tracks. As the industrialization of agriculture drives small farmers off the land, more people come to the town to work. More small businesses appear. The river is only used for sewage disposal.

Soon other tracks begin to contest with the railroad for moving goods. As more people have automobiles, highways are improved. The factories have more and more unpleasant slum areas surrounding them. People continue to move to the suburbs. Shipping of goods to and from the factory changes from the railroad to the highway. The railroads begin to lose business and cut back on passenger service. More people are forced to use the highway. The highway is now the main artery for carrying goods into town and the railroad is no longer vital to the town's functions. It becomes secondary to the life of the city as the river did before it. However, the railroad and river still have an influence on the city's development because their land stretches through the city's center and is very valuable even though it houses only slums and decaying warehouses.

The factories shift from coal to oil and electricity for power, as machines become smaller and more efficient. The town makes its center along the highway. It spreads in a haphazard fashion in all directions for it is neither restrained by the banks of the river or held together by the railroad tracks.

Because of the complexity of its functions, we will look at the modern city as a series of games rather than one all-encompassing game in itself.

At this point in the town's development our first game begins. The highway runs through the town which has office buildings and stores at its center. The factories are at the edge of town, and beyond this is farmland. There are pockets of slums in the center of the town — along the railway line and on the waterfront. The objective of the first part of the game, in which the form of the city takes shape, is to maximize one's wealth.

Materials

A pair of dice, play money. Cut out and construct the game pieces and city plan as shown on the drawings. Draw a line for the highway, for the railroad, and for the river. Place the different squares around the highway in ascending values from the town center as shown. Farmland is placed on the outskirts of the town according to the number of players involved.

As the land values of squares change, squares of corresponding values are substituted. Use either colored or textured paper or cardboard to indicate the value of squares. The map may be made any size to accommodate any number of players.

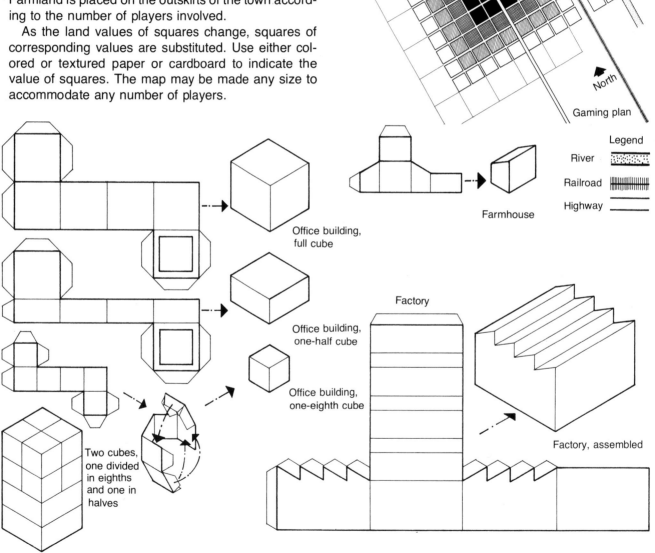

North

Gaming plan

Legend

River

Railroad

Highway

Office building, full cube

Office building, one-half cube

Office building, one-eighth cube

Two cubes, one divided in eighths and one in halves

Farmhouse

Factory

Factory, assembled

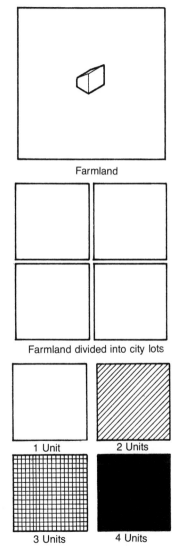

Farmland

Farmland divided into city lots

| 1 Unit | 2 Units |
| 3 Units | 4 Units |

City land

Players consist of businessmen (office building owners), industrialists (factory owners), farmers (who own farmland adjacent to the city), and an entrepreneur who is a land speculator. The entrepreneur also acts as banker.

Rules

The game is begun by rolling the dice. The player with the highest number is allowed first choice of business units and the land on which they are to be located. After investments are made and businesses purchased and placed on their squares, the dice are rolled to indicate business conditions for that year. The banker makes payoffs and collects penalties.

There is then a period of negotiation. Players may buy land from the entrepreneur or make deals with each other. After the negotiations are concluded, the dice are rolled for high number again and the next round of play begins.

Each player, except for the farmers, is given 50 units of money. He can buy either office buildings or factories, or both. Farmers do not have money: they have land, which they can sell to the entrepreneur who divides it into town lots and sells it to the businessmen. All farmers have an equal amount of land. Farmland does not come into play until it is bought from the farmers by the entrepreneur. Farmers can sell part of their land immediately, if the entrepreneur wants to buy it, and either buy business pieces or wait to see in which direction the city will develop and thus possibly increase the value of their land.

1. Office buildings cost 8 units per full cube. Half and one-eighth cubes may also be purchased. Factories cost 16 units.

2. Land values are as indicated from 1 to 4 units. Values cannot increase beyond 4 or drop below 1. Minimal value of farmland when it becomes part of the city is 1.

3. Office buildings pay the land value times half the unit cost in profit to their owners. Profits increase as office building units are added to the land.

4. Factory buildings pay a fixed profit of 10 units no matter what the value of the land they occupy.

5. Factory units occupy one entire square. If the factory owner wants to increase his profits, he must buy more land and another factory.

6. The entrepreneur has no money at the beginning of the game. When players buy land, they pay the entrepreneur for it. This is the entrepreneur's capital. He can only make money by buying land from the farmers, dividing it into city squares, and selling it to the businessmen. He can charge as much for the land as the businessmen are willing to pay. If the entrepreneur offers them cheaper land on the outskirts of the city, the businessmen can move there to escape the possibility that the center of the city will become so crowded that their businesses become unprofitable.

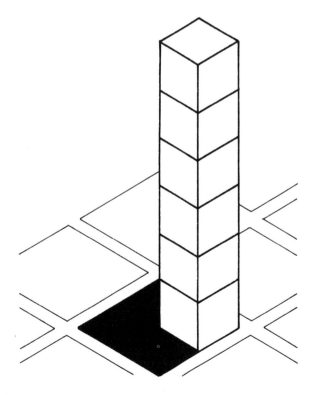

7. Office building cubes can be stacked as high as the businessman wants, up to 6 cubes.

8. Each office owner pays the unit value of the land square as rent for each building he has on it. If he builds higher, his rent does not increase.

9. Land can be improved. If a businessman wants to pay 20 units, he improves the land value of that particular square by 1 unit — up to a value of 4. If four businessmen are in the same square; they can improve the land value by cooperating and each contributing 5 units.

10. When all the land in the center of the town (squares valued at 4 units) is built up to an average of 128 units for each square (16 full-sized office cubes per square), all the squares adjacent to the town center increase in value by 1 point. The squares next to these also increase by 1 point. Farmland increases in potential value but this value cannot be realized until it is sold to the entrepreneur. As city land increases in value, players will try to make deals with the entrepreneur to influence him in buying farmland as a source of cheaper land.

It will become apparent that when land values increase in the center of the city, it is unprofitable for certain businesses to remain there.

11. Players can move their business. A player can buy another piece of land and move his business or relinquish his business piece and put a more lucrative business in its place.

12. Business pieces can be bought from the banker only.

13. The cost of moving a business piece is one-half the value of the piece, 8 units for a factory and 4 units for each office building.

14. When land increases in value, players must pay the increased value of the land as rent.

15. Farmers can subdivide their land and place business pieces on it if they can raise the money to do so. They do not have to pay rent for businesses on their own land.

The businessmen and factory owners expect to collect profits on their businesses. If they have guessed correctly, the center of town will continue to expand, business will improve, and the town will be prosperous. The businessmen might wish to speed the growth of the city by improving the value of the land themselves, which will result in increased profits.

The farmers want to sell their land at the best price. They will then use the money to either buy business pieces and rent land in the center of the city or subdivide the remainder of their land and place business pieces on it themselves.

Game Card *(dice combinations 2 to 12)*

2 — If there are 4-square-block areas in the city containing buildings aggregating over 120 units, then the city has become too crowded in this area. Land value is decreased by 1 unit in the 4-block area.

3 — A rumor that a new government highway will be constructed across the river to the east. All land on the riverbank increases 1 unit in value. Land to the west of the highway loses 1 unit in value.

4 — The rumor of the government highway proves to be false. Land values revert back to their original value. Land west of the highway increases 1 unit. Land along the river drops in value 1 unit.

5 — Factories suffer a shortage of markets. Half the labor force is laid off and factories pay only one-half their value.

6 — The river floods. All property bordering the riverbank decreases 1 unit in value. All buildings decrease one-half in value in this area due to flood damage.

7 — The city decides to build a sewage plant upriver and clean up the waterfront. All property owners are taxed 1 credit unit. Waterfront property increases two units in value along the river.

8 — An increase in demand for factory products means that the factories will pay double for this play.

9 — A downturn in business means that office buildings are only half rented. They pay half revenues for the squares they occupy and earn one-half profits.

10 — A bad farm year makes the farmer desperate for capital. Each farmer must sell off one-quarter of his land. The entrepreneur negotiates the price with him.

11 — A rumor that land to the east of the city will be opened up for development drives all land values in the center of town down 1 unit. The developer must sell his central city land for 1 unit less.

12 — Bad business year. Land values decline one unit per square in all areas.

The Game of People Working In the City

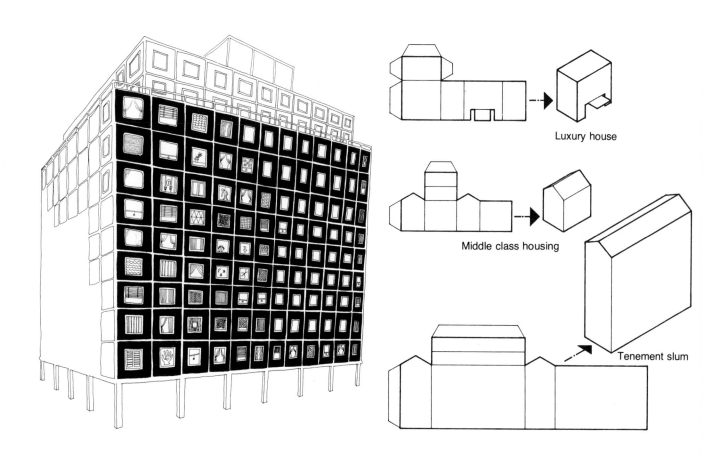

Luxury house

Middle class housing

Tenement slum

After the land-profit game has been played and the form of the city has taken shape, another element can be added to the game — that of the people who live and work in the city. The objective is to survive in the city, better one's living conditions, and maximize wealth.

Materials

Game markers for slums, middle-class housing, and luxury housing.

Players

Players consist of executives, office workers, and unskilled laborers.

Rules

This game is an extension of the previous game. The same rules and procedures apply. Unskilled laborers live in the slums and work primarily in the factories. A very few of them work in the office buildings. The office workers work in the office buildings. The executives work in the office buildings.

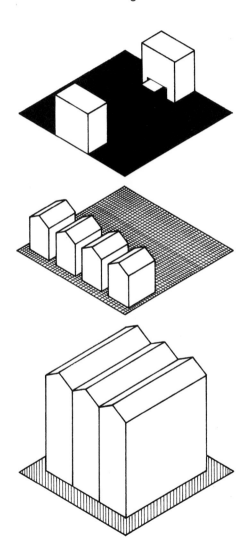

The businessmen can now buy housing pieces and use them on the land as they did office buildings and factories.

1. Slum units cost 2 credits. Middle-class housing for office workers costs 2 credits. Luxury housing units for executives cost 2 credits.

2. Luxury housing has 20 tenants, 2 to a unit, 2 housing units to a square. Middle-class housing has 40 tenants, 4 to a unit, 4 housing units to a square. There are 80 tenement dwellers, 8 to a unit, 3 housing units to a square.

3. The executives earn 8 credit units, office workers earn 4 credit units, and tenement dwellers earn 2 credit units.

4. The executives and office workers pay one-quarter of their earnings to the landlord as rent. Tenement dwellers pay one-third of their earnings as rent.

5. Each landlord pays the unit value of the square as rent.

6. Factories and office buildings cannot pay profits unless there are people to work in them. Each office building must have 1 luxury apartment dweller, 4 office workers and 2 unskilled workers. Each factory must have 8 unskilled workers.

7. If any of the tenants have to travel more than 10 squares to reach their work destination, they lose their work efficiency and earn half as much in credit units. If they have to travel more than 20 squares, they cannot get to work. They stay home and half their wages are paid as welfare. The businessmen must therefore arrange businesses and housing close enough together so that the workers can commute to work. Each businessman is taxed an equal percentage of his earnings to pay for workers who cannot get to work.

If there are not enough workers to work in the offices and factories, more players representing tenants can be added or use more tenants for each player.

The game can be played with two variations — one with more people than jobs, which will work out to the advantage of the businessmen, or the other with more jobs than workers, which is to the advantage of the tenants.

The Game of City Government

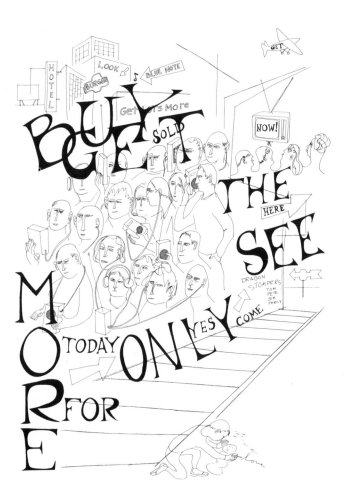

Materials

Use the same materials constructed for the first two sections of the game. The objective of this game is to make the city work efficiently.

Players

One or more players — representing the city government.

Rules

The government is represented by one or more players. If there is more than one player, they must act in agreement. The player or players acting as the government can be voted into or out of office by a majority of the other players.

1. The government is elected by the players with a secret ballot. These can be slips of paper, which are marked, folded, and counted by the player who has been acting as banker.

2. Each candidate must pay 50 credit units for the privilege of running. These credit units are the city treasury, which is used by the government.

3. A player can be supported by other players who will help him pay the campaign fund, or he can be a player who runs for office on his own.

4. The government can be voted out of office after 4 rounds of play if two-thirds of the other players are in disagreement with its policies.

5. The government collects taxes and with this money tries to improve the city by solving some of its problems. For example, the government might find that public housing is needed in certain parts of the city. If so, it buys land from the entrepreneur, as well as housing units. It places the housing on the land and charges rent for it.

6. The government can pay to increase the value of the land in certain parts of the city to improve business or alleviate congestion.

NON ....☐

YA..☐

NEIN ....☐

YES..☐

NO.........................☐

HIP.☐

SQUARE.....................☐

7. The government taxes the players to finance its ideas for improving the city. At this point it is best that the players themselves devise ways to improve their city to make it function well. They might think of introducing rapid-transit systems, or developing suburban housing near the factories so that tenement dwellers can have a better life and get to and from work more easily.

The government might consider installing a purification plant at the waterfront and turning the river into a public park which would improve the life of the city.

The railroad tracks still stretch through the center of the city. The land is no longer used by trains. This land might be used for urban renewal if all the players vote to buy it with their taxes.

Any number of solutions for the city are open to the players. The form of the city will depend upon their decisions. If they continue to maximize their wealth and each player works for himself against the others, the city will become harder and harder to operate and eventually it will not work at all.

89

You Design A City

We have seen thus far that human settlements are formed by the games people play with their lives. We have also found that there are a great number of rules possible for living together and that these rules determine the form of the settlement. If you wanted to design a city, what rules would you make? For example, what would a city be like if the people did not fight with each other over their food like prehistoric hunters, did not compete against each other for grain or cattle like primitive villagers, did not slaughter each other for land as they did in barbarian Europe, or contest against each other for the right to live and do business like the merchants and the lords in the medieval city? What would the city be like if its people did not have to cluster close together for protection against hostile members of another race and culture like the New England village, or did not have to compete for the right to sell cattle or grow food like the people of the cattle town?

You have seen that the effort to maximize one's wealth through personal profits and land speculation creates all sorts of problems in the modern city, and that it is difficult to administer such a city.

The final game of human settlements is to be designed by you. You must compose your own rules from what you have learned by playing the games in this book. Design the rules for a game that will result in a city you would like to live in.

Review the games of the book and find the rules that made life more difficult than it already was, from the time of prehistoric hunters to the modern city dweller, and then consider alternatives.

This does not mean that there will be no competition. Everyone likes games and games are based on competition. But competition does not have to be destructive. We compete in checkers, in athletics, in science, and in art. These are competitions that we all enjoy. There is not much enjoyment in the competition of fighting, land speculation, and political maneuvering. At least, the losers do not seem to enjoy such games nearly as much as the winners, and there are invariably more losers than winners. In some games, such as war, there are no winners at all.

We have seen that people who did not change their ideas when conditions changed, and did not adapt to new circumstances, did not survive. Modern cities may be facing such a crisis.

We might ask ourselves, does it make any sense to have cowboys in lunar laboratories? When men and women work in outer space, they do not wear six-guns. Space pioneers wear no arms at all. The bow and arrow, the sword, the spear, the six-gun, and the aerial bomb are old ideas that people in today's world must discard if we are to survive.

Design your own game of a modern human settlement. Play by the rules you devise and see what the results will be. It is easier to explore the future with a game of cardboard models than it is to build up and tear down buildings made of concrete and steel.

Materials

Cardboard markers of any size and shape you desire, on a gaming board of your own choosing.

Players

Yourself and the whole wide world.

Rules

These are to be made by you. The following are merely suggestions.

1. A city should be a place of great variety. We have seen the many ways people have found to live together. Choices preserve human settlements, restrictions destroy them.

2. Should the best parts of the land which man has always enjoyed, such as riverbanks, green meadows, and stands of trees, be covered by factories and office buildings or should they be used for schools, playgrounds, and parks?

3. Can a human settlement afford private property? Isn't land too valuable to be owned by anyone who can afford it? Should a land bank be created where poorly used city land could be loaned to those who demonstrate a better use for it, as free land was given to the homesteaders of the old west?

4. Should decisions affecting all the players be made by one of them? You will probably find that some decisions should be made by all and some should be individual. For example, a concrete building foundation will last for five hundred years and a refrigerator will last for only five. The things that come close to individuals — the kind of spaces they live in, the style of their houses, the life-style they choose, whether they build their own house, or whether they have someone build it for them — should perhaps be individual decisions. But, where to place major buildings, where to locate city services, and what kinds of services to provide — these questions should be decided by everyone.

These are only some of the rules you might consider. It is not easy to design the game rules for a satisfying human settlement; but certainly, it must be easier than living under the rules we have made in the past.

Bibliography

Abt, Clark C. *Serious Games*. New York: The Viking Press, 1970.

Argan, Giulio C. *Military Considerations in City Planning: Fortifications*. New York: George Braziller, 1972.

Bell, Colin and Rose. *City Fathers — Town Planning in Britain from Roman Times to 1900*. New York: Frederick A. Praeger, 1969.

Benevolo, Leonardo. *The Origins of Modern Town Planning*. Cambridge: M.I.T. Press, 1971.

Fraser, Douglas. *Village Planning in the Primitive World*. New York: George Braziller, 1968.

Hindley, Geoffrey. *Castles of Europe*. Feltham, Middlesex: Paul Hamlyn Limited, 1968.

Martin, Paul. *Arms and Armour,* Rutland, Vermont and Tokyo: Charles E. Tuttle Company, Inc., 1967.

Mumford, Lewis. *The City in History*. New York: Harcourt, Brace and World, Inc., 1961.

Pirenne, Henri, *Medieval Cities*. Garden City: Doubleday Anchor Books, 19

Prussin, Labelle. *Architecture in Northern Ghana*. University of California Press, 1969.

Saalman, Howard. *Medieval Cities*. New York: George Braziller, 1968.

Sandstrom, Gosta E. *Man the Builder*. New York: McGraw-Hill, 1970.

Simons, Gerald and the editors of Time-Life Books. *Barbarian Europe*. (Great Ages of Man Series). New York: Time-Life Books, 1968.

Index